Advancing Vocabulary Skills

Short Version

Fifth Edition

Advancing Vocabulary Skills

Short Version

Fifth Edition

Eliza Comodromos
Paul Langan

Additional Materials from Townsend Press

PRINT

Reading Skills

Groundwork for College Reading with Phonics
Groundwork for College Reading
Ten Steps to Building College Reading Skills
Ten Steps to Improving College Reading Skills
Ten Steps to Advancing College Reading Skills
Ten Steps to Mastering College Reading Skills

Vocabulary Skills

Vocabulary Basics
Groundwork for a Better Vocabulary
Building Vocabulary Skills
Building Vocabulary Skills, Short Version
Improving Vocabulary Skills
Improving Vocabulary Skills, Short Version
Advancing Vocabulary Skills
Advancing Vocabulary Skills, Short Version
Advanced Word Power

English, Grammar, and Writing Skills

English Essentials
The Reading-Writing Connection
The Advanced Reading-Writing Connection
Voices and Values: A Reader for Writers

Print Supplement (for Most Books)

Instructor's Edition

DIGITAL

Reading Skills

Ten Steps Plus
Ten Steps Plus LE, Limited Edition
College Reading Essentials Plus

Vocabulary Skills

Vocabulary Plus

English, Grammar, and Writing Skills

English Essentials Plus
Reading-Writing Plus
Reading-Writing Plus LE, Limited Edition

Digital Assessments

College Reading Test (4 forms)
Basic Written English Test (2 forms)
Vocabulary Placement Test

Digital Supplements (for Most Books)

Instructor's Manual and Test Bank
PowerPoints
eBooks

Printed in the United States of America
9 8 7 6 5 4 3 2 1

ISBN-13 (Student Edition): 978-1-59194-539-0
ISBN-13 (Instructor's Edition): 978-1-59194-540-6

Send book orders and requests for desk copies or supplements to:

Townsend Press Book Center
439 Kelley Drive
West Berlin, New Jersey 08091

For even faster service, contact us in any of the following ways:

By telephone: 1-800-772-6410
By fax: 1-800-225-8894
By email: cs@townsendpress.com
Through our website: www.townsendpress.com

Contents

NOTE: Each of the chapters presents ten words apiece. For ease of reference, the title of the selection that closes each chapter is included.

Unit Four

Appendixes

Preface: To the Instructor

Words have power. They express our emotions, convey our ideas, articulate our opinions, and reveal our thoughts. Students without an expansive vocabulary are challenged when asked to do these tasks. Furthermore, weak vocabularies limit students' understanding of what they read and the clarity of what they write. Many teachers tell us that their students' vocabularies are inadequate for academic demands.

Advancing Vocabulary Skills, Short Version aims to correct this problem. Spanning 20 chapters divided into 4 units, it teaches 200 important words. Here are the book's distinctive features:

1 **An intensive words-in-context approach.** Studies show that students learn words best by reading them repeatedly in different contexts, not through rote memorization. The book gives students an intensive in-context experience by presenting each word in *at least* **six** different contexts. Each chapter takes students through a productive sequence of steps:

- Students infer the meaning of each word by considering two sentences in which it appears and then choosing from multiple-choice options.
- On the basis of their inferences, students identify each word's meaning in a matching test. They are then in a solid position to deepen their knowledge of a word.
- Finally, they strengthen their understanding of a word by using it three times: in two sentence-length practices and in one longer passage. Each encounter with a word brings it closer to becoming part of the student's permanent word bank.

2 **Abundant practice.** Along with extensive practice in each chapter, there are a crossword puzzle and a set of unit tests at the end of every five-chapter unit. The puzzle and tests reinforce students' knowledge of the words in each unit. In addition, subsequent chapters revisit words from earlier chapters (repeated words are marked with small circles, like this°), allowing for more reinforcement. Last, there are supplementary tests in the *Instructor's Manual and Test Bank,* which is available in the Learning Center to instructors as a downloadable PDF. All this practice means that students learn in the surest possible way: by working closely and repeatedly with each word. And if you prefer even more practice, *Vocabulary Plus*—our digital word-building program—is available. See page viii for details.

3 **Controlled feedback and opportunities for independent learning.** The opening activity in each chapter gives students three multiple-choice options to help them decide on the meaning of a given word. This activity also helps students complete the matching exercise that is the second activity of each chapter. A limited answer key at the back of the book then provides answers for the third activity in the chapter. All these features enable students to take an active role in their own learning.

4 **Focus on essential words.** A good deal of time and research went into selecting the words and word parts in each book in the Vocabulary Series. Word frequency lists were consulted, along with word banks in a wide range of vocabulary books. In addition, the authors and editors each prepared their own lists based on their teaching experience. A lengthy process of data consolidation followed by group discussion then led to final decisions about the words and word parts that would be most helpful for students on each level.

5 **Appealing content.** Dull practice materials work against learning. On the other hand, meaningful, lively, and at times even funny sentences and passages can spark students' attention and enhance their grasp of the material. For this reason, a great deal of effort was put into creating sentences and passages with both widespread appeal and solid context support. We have tried throughout to make the practice materials truly enjoyable for teachers and students alike.

6 **Clear format.** The book has been designed so that its very format contributes to the learning process. Each chapter consists of two two-page spreads. In the first spread (see pages 8–9), students can easily refer to all ten words in context while working on the matching activity, which provides a clear meaning for each word. In the second spread (see pages 10–11), students can refer to a box that shows all ten words while they work through the fill-in activities on these pages.

7 **Supplementary materials.**

a A convenient *Instructor's Edition* is available at no charge to educators using the book. It is identical to the student book except that it contains answers to all of the activities and tests.

b A downloadable electronic (PDF) *Instructor's Manual and Test Bank* is also offered to instructors at no charge in the Learning Center (www.townsendpress.net). This digital supplement contains a general vocabulary placement test, along with a pretest and a posttest for the entire book as well as for each of its five units. It also includes teaching guidelines, suggested syllabi, an answer key, and an additional mastery test for each chapter and for each unit.

c *PowerPoint presentations* are available for this book and may be downloaded at no charge from the Learning Center. Educators must have an approved instructor account to access this material. The PowerPoints can be used in class to give students a visual introduction to the words and word parts of each chapter in their text.

d *eBooks* of student editions of all titles in the Vocabulary Series are available in the Learning Center. These eBooks serve as a free reference copy of the class text whenever educators need it. To learn more about the various digital supplements and other products, visit www.townsendpress.com or contact Customer Service (see below).

8 **Realistic pricing.** As with the previous editions, the goal has been to offer the highest possible quality at the lowest possible price. While *Advancing Vocabulary Skills* is comprehensive enough to serve as a primary text, its modest price also makes it an inexpensive supplement.

9 **One in a sequence of books.** The most fundamental book in the Townsend Press vocabulary series is *Vocabulary Basics*. It is followed by *Groundwork for a Better Vocabulary* (a slightly more advanced basic text) and then by the three main books in the series: *Building Vocabulary Skills* (also a basic text), *Improving Vocabulary Skills* (an intermediate text), and *Advancing Vocabulary Skills* (a more advanced text). The most advanced book in the Townsend Press vocabulary series is *Advanced Word Power*. There are also short versions of the *Building*, *Improving*, and *Advancing* books. Suggested grade levels for the books can be found on our website or in the *Instructor's Manual*. Together, the books can help create a vocabulary foundation that will make any student a better reader, writer, and thinker.

10 **Digital options.** Looking for a paperless way to teach vocabulary? We've got it. ***Vocabulary Plus*** is a comprehensive online vocabulary program powered by TP's bestselling 9-book Vocabulary Series. *Vocabulary Plus* brings **all** the content of our famously clear, user-friendly texts directly to your tablet, smartphone, or computer. Offering traditional class-based approaches or an adaptive independent study mode, *Vocabulary Plus* can be purchased as an individual subscription, through an institutional license, or as part of a discounted textbook bundle. Contact Customer Service at cs@townsendpress.com or call (800) 772-6410 for purchase options. Two-week free trials are available!

Notes on the Fifth Edition

A number of enhancements have been made to the fifth edition of *Advancing Vocabulary Skills, Short Version:*

- **An abundance of new and resequenced items.** As always, a good deal of content throughout the book has been replaced with brand new items to ensure the text works as clearly and effectively as possible with students. And items in both Sentence Checks have been resequenced from the previous edition. We listened to your requests!
- **Contemporary design.** Page format, design elements, and even the cover have been updated to reflect the vibrancy and energy of today's students and classrooms. While these visuals have been updated, the acclaimed clarity and readability of the previous editions have been preserved.
- **Thirty new photographs.** To engage today's visual learners, a full-color photograph has been added to the Final Check passage in each chapter.
- **General freshening for today's audiences.** The Vocabulary Series is popular in colleges as well as in middle and high schools. To reflect this diverse audience, practice materials, passages, and test items were freshened and updated for maximum appeal, relevance, and effectiveness for readers of all ages.

Acknowledgments

Having served as assistant editors for the Vocabulary Series for two decades, we are grateful to the mighty editorial crew at Townsend Press for their leadership, expertise, and patience. We stand on the shoulders of giants. Special gratitude goes to John Langan, Judy Nadell, Barbara Solot, Carole Mohr, and Sherrie L. Nist for their work on the book's previous editions. We would also like to thank Beth Johnson and Tanya Savory for their invaluable content contributions and Stéphane Descamps and Noémie Fior for the page design and layout of the fifth edition. A special shout-out goes to Bruce Kenselaar, who is responsible for the exciting new cover art and interior graphic design. Most of all, we continue to receive invaluable contributions from Janet Goldstein, editor extraordinaire, who has lent her exceptional and impeccable editing skills to this and so many Townsend Press publications. And a final tip of the hat goes to Anna, Sophia, and Yianni, our beloved budding wordsmiths.

Eliza Comodromos
Paul Langan

Introduction

Why Vocabulary Development Counts

You have probably often heard it said, "Building vocabulary is important." Maybe you've politely nodded in agreement and then forgotten the matter. But it would be fair for you to ask, "*Why* is vocabulary development important? Provide some evidence." Here are four compelling arguments:

1. Common sense tells you what many research studies have shown as well: **vocabulary is a basic part of reading comprehension**. Simply put, if you don't know enough words, you are going to have trouble understanding what you read. An occasional word may not stop you, but if there are too many words you don't know, comprehension will suffer. The content of textbooks is often challenging enough; you don't want to spend extra time on understanding the words that express that content.

2. **Vocabulary is a major part of almost every standardized test**, including reading achievement tests, high-school exit exams, college entrance exams, and armed forces and vocational placement tests. Test developers know that vocabulary is a key measure of both one's learning and one's ability to learn. It is for this reason that they include a separate vocabulary section as well as a reading comprehension section. The more words you know, then, the better you are likely to do on such important tests.

3. Studies have indicated that **students with strong vocabularies are more successful in school**. And one widely known study found that **a good vocabulary, more than any other factor, was common to people enjoying successful careers in life**. Words are, in fact, the tools not only of better reading, but of better writing, speaking, listening, and thinking as well. The more words you have at your command, the more effective your communication can be, and the more influence you can have on the people around you.

4. **In today's world, a good vocabulary counts more than ever.** Far fewer people work on farms or in factories. Far more are in jobs that provide services or process information. More than ever, words are the tools of our trade: words we use in reading, writing, listening, and speaking. Furthermore, experts say that tomorrow's workers will be called on to change jobs and learn new skills at an ever-increasing pace. The keys to survival and success will be the abilities to communicate skillfully and learn quickly. A solid vocabulary is essential for both of these skills.

Clearly, the evidence is overwhelming that building vocabulary is crucial. The question then becomes, "What is the best way of going about it?"

Words in Context: The Key to Vocabulary Development

Memorizing lists of words is a traditional method of vocabulary development. However, you are likely to forget such memorized lists quickly. Studies show that to master a word (or a word part), you must see and use it in various contexts. By working actively and repeatedly with a word, you greatly increase the chance of really learning it.

The following activity will make clear how this book is organized and how it uses a words-in-context approach. Answer the questions or fill in the missing words in the spaces provided.

Inside Front Cover and Contents

Turn to the inside front cover.

- The inside front cover provides a ______________________ that will help you pronounce all the vocabulary words in the book.

Now turn to the table of contents on pages v–vi.

- How many chapters are in the book? ________
- Four sections follow the last chapter. The first of these sections provides a limited answer key, the second gives helpful information on using ____________________________, the third contains ____________________________________, and the fourth is a list of the 200 words in the book.

Vocabulary Chapters

Turn to Chapter 1 on pages 8–11. This chapter, like all the others, consists of five parts:

- The ***first part*** of the chapter, on pages 8–9, is titled ____________________________________.

The left-hand column lists the ten words. Under each **boldfaced** word is its ____________________ (in parentheses). For example, the pronunciation of *detriment* is ______________________. For a guide to pronunciation, see the inside front cover as well as "Dictionary Use" on page 131.

Below the pronunciation guide for each word is its part of speech. The part of speech shown for *detriment* is ____________. The vocabulary words in this book are mostly nouns, adjectives, and verbs. **Nouns** are words used to name something—a person, place, thing, or idea. Familiar nouns include *teacher, city, hat,* and *truth.* **Adjectives** are words that describe nouns, as in the following word pairs: *former* teacher, *large* city, *red* hat, *whole* truth. All of the **verbs** in this book express an action of some sort. They tell what someone or something is doing. Common verbs include *sing, separate, support,* and *imagine.*

To the right of each word are two sentences that will help you understand its meaning. In each sentence, the **context**—the words surrounding the boldfaced word—provides clues you can use to figure out the definition. There are four common types of context clues: examples, synonyms, antonyms, and the general sense of the sentence. Each is briefly described below.

1 Examples

A sentence may include examples that reveal what an unfamiliar word means. For instance, take a look at the following sentence from Chapter 1 for the word *scrupulous*:

> The judge was **scrupulous** about never accepting a bribe or allowing a personal threat to influence his decisions.

The sentence provides two examples of what makes the judge scrupulous. The first is that he never accepted a bribe. The second is that the judge did not allow personal threats to influence his decisions. What do these two examples have in common? The answer to that question will tell you what *scrupulous* means. Look at the answer choices below, and in the answer space provided, write the letter of the one you think is correct.

___ *Scrupulous* means A. ethical. B. economical. C. unjust.

Both of the examples given in the sentences about the judge tell us that he is honest, or ethical. So if you wrote *A*, you chose the correct answer.

2 Synonyms

Synonyms are words that mean the same or almost the same as another word. For example, the words *joyful, happy*, and *delighted* are synonyms—they all mean about the same thing. Synonyms serve as context clues by providing the meaning of an unknown word that is nearby. The sentence below from Chapter 2 provides a synonym clue for *collaborate*.

> When Sarah and I were asked to **collaborate** on a science fair project, we found it difficult to work together.

Instead of using *collaborate* twice, the author used a synonym in the second part of the sentence. Find that synonym, and then choose the letter of the correct answer from the choices below.

___ *Collaborate* means A. to compete. B. to stop work. C. to act as a team.

The author uses two terms to express what Sarah and the speaker had to do: *collaborate* and *work together*. Therefore, *collaborate* must be another way of saying "work together." (The author could have written, "Sarah and I were asked to work together.") Since *work together* can also mean "act as a team," the correct answer is *C*.

3 Antonyms

Antonyms are words with opposite meanings. For example, *help* and *harm* are antonyms, as are *work* and *rest.* Antonyms serve as context clues by providing the opposite meaning of an unknown word. For instance, the sentence below from Chapter 1 provides an antonym clue for the word *gregarious*.

> My **gregarious** brother loves parties, but my shy sister prefers to be alone.

The author is contrasting the brother's and sister's different personalities, so we can assume that *gregarious* and *shy* have opposite, or contrasting, meanings. Using that contrast as a clue, write the letter of the answer that you think best defines *gregarious*.

___ *Gregarious* means A. attractive. B. outgoing. C. humorous.

The correct answer is *B*. Because *gregarious* is the opposite of *shy*, it must mean "outgoing."

4 General Sense of the Sentence

Even when there is no example, synonym, or antonym clue in a sentence, most of the time you can still figure out the meaning of an unfamiliar word. For example, look at the sentence from Chapter 1 for the word *detriment*.

> Smoking is a **detriment** to your health. It's estimated that each cigarette you smoke will shorten your life by one and a half minutes.

After studying the context carefully, you should be able to figure out the connection between smoking and health. That will be the meaning of *detriment*. Write the letter of your choice.

___ *Detriment* means A. an aid. B. a discovery. C. a disadvantage.

Since the sentence says that each cigarette will shorten the smoker's life by one and a half minutes, it is logical to conclude that smoking has a bad effect on health. Thus answer *C* is correct.

By looking closely at the pair of sentences provided for each word, as well as the answer choices, you should be able to decide on the meaning of a word. As you figure out each meaning, you are working actively with the word. You are creating the groundwork you need to understand and to remember the word. *Getting involved with the word and developing a feel for it, based upon its use in context, is the key to word mastery.*

It is with good reason, then, that the directions at the top of page 8 tell you to use the context to figure out each word's ______________________. Doing so deepens your sense of the word and prepares you for the next activity.

- The ***second part*** of the chapter, on page 9, is titled ______________________________________.

According to research, it is not enough to see a word in context. At a certain point, it is helpful as well to see the meaning of a word. The matching activity provides that meaning, but it also makes you look for and think about that meaning. In other words, it continues the active learning that is your surest route to learning and remembering a word.

Note the caution that follows this activity. Do not proceed any further until you are sure that you know the correct meaning of each word as used in context.

Keep in mind that a word may have more than one meaning. In fact, some words have quite a few meanings. (If you doubt it, try looking up the word *make* or *draw* in a dictionary.) In this book, you will focus on one common meaning for each vocabulary word. However, many of the words have additional meanings. For example, in Chapter 5, you will learn that *sham* means "a pretense or counterfeit; something meant to deceive," as in "Karen's apparent affection for Raul is a **sham**. He's rich, and she cares only about his money." If you then look up *sham* in the dictionary, you will discover that it has another meaning—"a cover used to change the appearance of an object," as in "Veronica bought shams so that her old pillows would match her new sofa." After you learn one common meaning of a word, you will find yourself gradually learning its other meanings in the course of your school and personal reading.

- The ***third part*** of the chapter, on page 10, is titled ______________________________________

Here are ten sentences that give you an opportunity to apply your understanding of the ten words. After inserting the words, check your answers in the limited answer key at the back of the book. Be sure to use the answer key as a learning tool only. Doing so will help you to master the words and to prepare for the last two activities and the unit tests, for which answers are not provided.

- The ***fourth and fifth parts*** of the chapter, on pages 10–11, are titled __________________________ and ___________________________.

Each practice tests you on all ten words, giving you two more chances to deepen your mastery. In the fifth part, you have the context of an entire passage in which you can practice applying the words.

At the bottom of the last page of this chapter is a box where you can enter your score for the final two checks. These scores should also be entered into the vocabulary performance chart located on the inside back cover of the book. To get your score, count the number of items that you answered correctly in each section. Then add a zero. For example, if you got seven answers right in Sentence Check 2, you would write "70" on the first line in the score box.

You now know, in a nutshell, how to proceed with the words in each chapter. Make sure that you do each page very carefully. *Remember that as you work through the activities, you are learning the words.*

How many times in all will you use each word? If you look, you'll see that each chapter gives you the opportunity to work with each word six times. Each "impression" adds to the likelihood that the word will become part of your active vocabulary. You will have further opportunities to use the word in the crossword puzzle and tests that end each unit and in the online exercises available at www.townsendpress.net.

In addition, many of the words are repeated in context in later chapters of the book. Such repeated words are marked with a small circle (°). For example, which words from Chapter 1 are repeated in the Final Check on page 15 of Chapter 2?

______________________ ______________________

Analogies

This book also offers practice in word analogies, yet another way to deepen your understanding of words. An **analogy** is a similarity between two things that are otherwise different. Doing an analogy question is a two-step process. First you have to figure out the relationship in a pair of words. Those words are written like this:

LEAF : TREE

What is the relationship between the two words above? The answer can be stated like this: A leaf is a part of a tree.

Next, you must look for a similar relationship in a second pair of words. Here is how a complete analogy question looks:

LEAF : TREE ::

A. pond : river
B. foot : shoe
C. page : book
D. beach : sky

And here is how the question can be read:

___ LEAF is to TREE as

A. *pond* is to *river.*
B. *foot* is to *shoe.*
C. *page* is to *book.*
D. *beach* is to *sky.*

To answer the question, you have to decide which of the four choices has a relationship similar to the first one. Check your answer by seeing if it fits in the same wording as you used to show the relationship between *leaf* and *tree:* A ___ is part of a ___. Which answer do you choose?

The correct answer is *C*. Just as a leaf is part of a tree, a page is part of a book. On the other hand, a pond is not part of a river, nor is a foot part of a shoe, nor is a beach part of the sky.

We can state the complete analogy this way: *Leaf* is to *tree* as *page* is to *book.*

Here's another analogy question to try. Begin by figuring out the relationship between the first two words.

___ COWARD : HERO ::

A. soldier : military
B. infant : baby
C. actor : famous
D. employer : employee

Coward and *hero* are opposite types of people. So you need to look at the other four pairs to see which has a similar relationship. When you think you have found the answer, check to see that the two words you chose can be compared in the same way as *coward* and *hero:* ___ and ___ are opposite types of people.

In this case, the correct answer is *D*; *employer* and *employee* are opposite kinds of people. (In other words, *coward* is to *hero* as *employer* is to *employee.*)

By now you can see that there are basically two steps to doing analogy items:

1 Find out the relationship of the first two words.
2 Find the answer that expresses the same type of relationship as the first two words have.

Now try one more analogy question on your own. Write the letter of the answer you choose in the space provided.

___ SWING : BAT ::

A. drive : car
B. run : broom
C. catch : bat
D. fly : butterfly

If you chose answer *A,* you were right. *Swing* is what we do with a *bat,* and *drive* is what we do with a *car.*

Here are some other relationships often found in analogies:

- **Synonyms:** freedom : liberty (*freedom* and *liberty* mean the same thing)
- **Item to category:** baseball : sport (baseball is one kind of sport)
- **Item to description:** school bus : yellow (*yellow* is a word that describes a school bus)
- **Producer to product:** singer: song (a singer is the person who produces a song)
- **Time sequence:** January : March (January occurs two months before March)

A Final Thought

The facts are in. A strong vocabulary is a source of power. Words can make you a better reader, writer, speaker, thinker, and learner. They can dramatically increase your chances of success in school and in your job.

But words will not come automatically. They must be learned in a program of regular study. If you commit yourself to learning words, and you work actively and honestly with the chapters in this book, you will not only enrich your vocabulary—you will enrich your life as well.

Unit One

Chapter 1

detriment	optimum
dexterous	ostentatious
discretion	scrupulous
facetious	sensory
gregarious	vicarious

Chapter 2

collaborate	rudimentary
despondent	scoff
instigate	squelch
resilient	venerate
retrospect	zealot

Chapter 3

ambiguous	inane
dissident	juxtapose
embellish	lethargy
fritter	sporadic
inadvertent	subsidize

Chapter 4

berate	maudlin
estrange	regress
euphoric	relinquish
impetuous	ubiquitous
infallible	zenith

Chapter 5

equivocate	propensity
fortuitous	reprehensible
impeccable	sham
liaison	solace
predisposed	solicitous

detriment	**optimum**
dexterous	**ostentatious**
discretion	**scrupulous**
facetious	**sensory**
gregarious	**vicarious**

Ten Words in Context

In the space provided, write the letter of the meaning closest to that of each **boldfaced** word. Use the context of the sentences to help you figure out each word's meaning.

1 detriment
(dĕ′trə-mənt)
-noun

- Brandi's face tattoo may be a **detriment** when she goes for a job interview.
- Smoking is a **detriment** to your health. It's estimated that each cigarette you smoke will shorten your life by one and a half minutes.

__ *Detriment* means A. an aid. B. a discovery. C. a disadvantage.

2 dexterous
(dĕks′tər-əs)
-adjective

- The juggler was so **dexterous** that he managed to keep five balls in motion at once.
- Although he has arthritis in his hands, Phil is very **dexterous**. For example, he builds detailed model airplanes.

__ *Dexterous* means A. skilled. B. educated. C. awkward.

3 discretion
(dĭ-skrĕsh′ən)
-noun

- Ali wasn't using much **discretion** when he passed a police car at eighty miles an hour.
- Small children haven't yet developed **discretion**. They ask embarrassing questions like "When will you be dead, Grandpa?"

__ *Discretion* means A. skill. B. good sense. C. courage.

4 facetious
(fə-sē′shəs)
-adjective

- For Father's Day, Mia bought her dad a t-shirt with this **facetious** slogan: "My Favorite Child Gave Me This Shirt."
- My boss always says, "You don't have to be crazy to work here, but it helps." I hope she's just being **facetious**.

__ *Facetious* means A. serious. B. uncertain. C. funny.

5 gregarious
(grĭ-gâr′ē-əs)
-adjective

- Melissa is so **gregarious** that she wants to be with other people even when she's studying.
- My **gregarious** brother loves parties, but my shy sister prefers to be alone.

__ *Gregarious* means A. attractive. B. outgoing. C. humorous.

6 optimum
(ŏp′tə-məm)
-adjective

- The road was so icy that the **optimum** driving speed was only about ten miles an hour.
- For the weary traveler, **optimum** hotel accommodations include a quiet room, a comfortable bed, and efficient room service.

__ *Optimum* means A. ideal. B. hopeful. C. questionable.

7 ostentatious
(ŏs′tən-tā′shəs)
-adjective

- My show-off aunt has some **ostentatious** jewelry, such as a gold bracelet that's so heavy she can hardly lift her arm.
- The lobby of that hotel is **ostentatious**, with fancy furniture, thick rugs, and tall flower arrangements. The guest rooms upstairs, however, are extremely plain.

___ *Ostentatious* means A. humble. B. showy. C. clean.

8 scrupulous
(skro͞o′pyə-ləs)
-adjective

- The judge was **scrupulous** about never accepting a bribe or allowing a personal threat to influence his decisions.
- The senator promised to run a **scrupulous** campaign, but her ads were filled with lies about her opponent's personal life.

___ *Scrupulous* means A. ethical. B. economical. C. unjust.

9 sensory
(sĕn′sə-rē)
-adjective

- Because our **sensory** experiences are interrelated, what we taste is greatly influenced by what we smell.
- A person in a flotation tank has almost no **sensory** stimulation. The tank is dark and soundproof, and the person floats in water at body temperature, unable to see or hear and scarcely able to feel anything.

___ *Sensory* means A. of the senses. B. social. C. intellectual.

10 vicarious
(vī-kâr′ē-əs)
-adjective

- I don't like to take risks myself, but I love the **vicarious** thrill of watching death-defying adventures in a movie.
- Reading allows people to have limitless **vicarious** experiences, such as traveling to other times, meeting famous people, or exploring distant worlds.

___ *Vicarious* means A. thorough. B. indirect. C. skillful.

Matching Words with Definitions

Following are definitions of the ten words. Clearly write or print each word next to its definition. The sentences above and on the previous page will help you decide on the meaning of each word.

1. ______________ Humorous; playfully joking
2. ______________ Meant to impress others; flashy
3. ______________ Best possible; most favorable; most desirable
4. ______________ Something that causes damage, harm, or loss
5. ______________ Experienced through the imagination; not experienced directly
6. ______________ Skillful in using the hands or body
7. ______________ Careful about moral standards; conscientious
8. ______________ Sociable; enjoying and seeking the company of others
9. ______________ Good judgment or tact in actions or speaking
10. ______________ Having to do with seeing, hearing, feeling, tasting, or smelling

CAUTION: Do not go any further until you are sure the above answers are correct. Then you can use the definitions to help you in the following practices. Your goal is eventually to know the words well enough so that you don't need to check the definitions at all.

Sentence Check 1

Using the answer line provided, complete each item below with the correct word from the box. Use each word once.

A. **detriment**	B. **dexterous**	C. **discretion**	D. **facetious**	E. **gregarious**
F. **optimum**	G. **ostentatious**	H. **scrupulous**	I. **sensory**	J. **vicarious**

_______________ 1. When his mother gave him money to buy new shoes, Joel was ___ about returning the change to her, even though it was only sixteen cents.

_______________ 2. My roommate used to be ___, but since he was mugged, he's begun to avoid people.

_______________ 3. Playing with blocks and puzzles makes children more ___ with their hands.

_______________ 4. A weak voice is a serious ___ to a stage actor's or actress's career.

_______________ 5. Any employee who wants to use ___ would simply ignore a piece of spinach on the boss's front tooth.

_______________ 6. My brother has given his extremely slow, lazy dog the ___ name "Speedy."

_______________ 7. Wandering through the bee-filled fields of red and yellow flowers was an amazing ___ experience, one that appealed to the eyes, ears, and nose.

_______________ 8. The ___ order in which to answer test questions is from easiest to most difficult, so that you can write the answers you know before time runs out.

_______________ 9. Do you think a spectator sport gives the fans ___ triumphs and defeats, or real ones?

_______________ 10. Jasmine wants to practice her vocabulary skills, so she's not just being ___ when she uses long words.

NOTE: Now check your answers to these items by turning to page 129. Going over the answers carefully will help you prepare for the next two practices, for which answers are not given.

Sentence Check 2

Using the answer lines provided, complete each item below with **two** words from the box. Use each word once.

____
_______________ 1–2. When you take vitamins, be sure to take only the recommended dose. Anything more than this ___ amount can be a dangerous ___ to your health.

____
_______________ 3–4. Tyra is being ___ when she says she's as ___ as a professional ballet dancer. That's her way of making fun of her own clumsiness.

____
_______________ 5–6. "You have to use ___ in choosing your friends," my father said. "If your associates are dishonest, people will think that you also may not be ___."

7–8. Our cousin in Nigeria writes great letters, filled with ___ details that give us a(n) ___ acquaintance with the sights and sounds of an African village.

9–10. My neighbors give a lot of parties, but not because they're ___. They just want to impress the guests with their ___ home and furnishings.

Final Check: *Apartment Problems*

Here is a final opportunity for you to strengthen your knowledge of the ten words. First read the following selection carefully. Then fill in each blank with a word from the box at the top of the previous page. (Context clues will help you figure out which word goes in which blank.) Use each word once.

Although I'm ordinarily a(n) (1)________________ person, I'm tempted to move into a cave, far from other people—and landlords. Okay, I admit that I didn't use enough (2)________________ in choosing apartments to rent. But does every one of them have to be a (3)________________ to my health, mental stability, and checkbook?

When I moved into my first apartment, I discovered that the previous tenant had already subleased the place to a very large family—of cockroaches. Although I kept trying, I was never (4)________________ enough to swat any of them; they were able to dodge all my blows. In time, they became so bold that they paraded across the kitchen floor in the daytime in a(n) (5)________________ manner meant to impress upon me how useless it was to try to stop them. As soon as I could, I moved out.

My second apartment was a(n) (6)________________ nightmare—the filth was hard on the eyes and the nose. The place even assaulted the ears, as the walls were as thin as cardboard. My neighbors played music until all hours. Since I was too poor to buy a stereo, I became a dedicated listener. I even attended some of the neighbors' parties, in a(n) (7)________________ way—with my ear to the wall. When my landlord found out, he tried to charge me seven dollars a day for entertainment, and he wasn't being (8)________________—he meant it. I moved again, hoping to find a decent, (9)________________ landlord.

I rented my last apartment because it was supposedly located in an area of (10)________________ safety, considering the rent I can afford. A week after I moved in, I came home to find the locks broken and my belongings all over the floor. On the dresser was an angry note: "What gives you the right to live in such a nice neighborhood and not have anything worth stealing?"

Maybe I should have stayed with the cockroaches. At least they were honest.

Scores Sentence Check 2 ________% Final Check ________%

Enter your scores above and in the **Vocabulary Performance Chart** on the inside back cover of the book.

collaborate
despondent
instigate
resilient
retrospect
rudimentary
scoff
squelch
venerate
zealot

Ten Words in Context

In the space provided, write the letter of the meaning closest to that of each **boldfaced** word. Use the context of the sentences to help you figure out each word's meaning.

1 collaborate (kə-lăb′ə-rāt′) *-verb*

- When Sarah and I were asked to **collaborate** on a science fair project, we found it difficult to work together.
- Several writers and editors have **collaborated** in preparing this vocabulary text, sharing their knowledge and skills.

__ *Collaborate* means A. to compete. B. to stop work. C. to act as a team.

2 despondent (dĭ-spŏn′dənt) *-adjective*

- Devon becomes **despondent** too easily. If he gets even one bad grade, he loses all hope of succeeding in school.
- For months after his wife died, Mr. Craig was **despondent**. No matter how hard they tried, his family and friends could not cheer him up.

__ *Despondent* means A. ill. B. depressed. C. angry.

3 instigate (ĭn′stə-gāt′) *-verb*

- The rock group's violent performance **instigated** a riot in the audience.
- An English captain named Robert Jenkins **instigated** a war in 1738 by displaying his pickled ear, which he said had been cut off by a Spanish patrol. The horrified British declared war on Spain—the "War of Jenkins' Ear."

__ *Instigate* means A. to prevent. B. to predict. C. to cause.

4 resilient (rĭ-zĭl′yənt) *-adjective*

- Children can be amazingly **resilient**. Even after a sad or frightening experience, they often bounce back to their normal cheerful selves.
- Plant life is **resilient**. For example, a few weeks after the Mount St. Helens volcano erupted in Washington in 1980, flowers were growing in the ashes.

__ *Resilient* means A. widespread. B. slow to recover. C. quick to recover.

5 retrospect (rĕt′rə-spĕkt′) *-noun*

- After hobbling around on her broken foot for a week before seeing a doctor, Mae then needed surgery. In **retrospect**, it's clear she should have gotten help sooner.
- When I took Ms. Klein's writing course, I thought she was too demanding. In **retrospect**, though, I realize that she taught me more than anyone else.

__ *In retrospect* means A. looking back. B. looking for excuses. C. looking ahead.

6 rudimentary (ro͞o′də-mĕn′tər-ē) *-adjective*

- Grammar books usually start with **rudimentary** skills, such as identifying nouns and verbs.
- I'm so used to adding and subtracting on a calculator that I've probably forgotten how to do those **rudimentary** mathematical calculations on my own.

__ *Rudimentary* means A. basic. B. intermediate. C. advanced.

7 scoff
(skŏf)
-verb

- Bystanders **scoffed** at the street musician playing a tune on a row of tin cans, but he seemed unaware that people were making fun of him.
- Tony **scoffed** at reports that a hurricane was coming until he saw the winds knocking down trees and overturning cars.

__ *Scoff at* means A. to laugh at. B. to watch. C. to take seriously.

8 squelch
(skwĕlch)
-verb

- My history teacher shot me a dirty look during class when I couldn't quite manage to **squelch** a burp.
- Decades of communism in Eastern Europe didn't **squelch** the desire for freedom. As soon as they could, the people in these countries began to form democracies.

__ *Squelch* means A. to encourage. B. to hold back. C. to release.

9 venerate
(vĕn′ər-āt′)
-verb

- The Tlingit Indians **venerate** the wolf and the raven, and their totem poles illustrate stories in praise of these animals.
- The guests at our dean's retirement banquet made it clear that they **venerated** her; when she entered the room, everyone rose.

__ *Venerate* means A. to pity. B. to honor. C. to remember.

10 zealot
(zĕl′ət)
-noun

- Annie, a **zealot** about health, runs a hundred miles a week and never lets a grain of sugar touch her lips.
- The Crusaders were Christian **zealots** during the Middle Ages who left their homes and families and went off to try to capture the Holy Land.

__ *Zealot* means A. an extremist. B. an observer. C. a doubter.

Matching Words with Definitions

Following are definitions of the ten words. Clearly write or print each word next to its definition. The sentences above and on the previous page will help you decide on the meaning of each word.

1. ____________________ To bring about by moving others to action; stir up
2. ____________________ Fundamental; necessary to learn first
3. ____________________ Able to recover quickly from harm, illness, or misfortune
4. ____________________ To work together on a project; cooperate in an effort
5. ____________________ A person totally devoted to a purpose or cause
6. ____________________ To silence or suppress; crush
7. ____________________ To respect deeply; revere
8. ____________________ Downhearted; hopeless; overwhelmed with sadness
9. ____________________ Reviewing the past; considering past events
10. ____________________ To make fun of; mock; refuse to take seriously

CAUTION: Do not go any further until you are sure the above answers are correct. Then you can use the definitions to help you in the following practices. Your goal is eventually to know the words well enough so that you don't need to check the definitions at all.

Sentence Check 1

Using the answer line provided, complete each item below with the correct word from the box. Use each word once.

A. collaborate	B. despondent	C. instigate	D. resilient	E. retrospect
F. rudimentary	G. scoff	H. squelch	I. venerate	J. zealot

________ 1. Mother Teresa, who devoted her life to helping the poor, is ___(e)d by Catholics worldwide. She became a saint in 2016.

________ 2. Dawn is a ___ about gun control. She has walked for miles in protest marches and stood in the rain for hours during demonstrations.

________ 3. The novel *Uncle Tom's Cabin*, which exposed the horrors of slavery, helped to ___ the American Civil War.

________ 4. Jaime was ___ over the death of his dog, his companion for fourteen years.

________ 5. My ability to speak Spanish is ___, but I can at least manage to ask directions or order a meal.

________ 6. Athletes need to be ___. After a defeat, an individual or a team must be able to come back and fight for victory the next time.

________ 7. Since I'd like to be a photographer, I can see, in ___, that I would have gained valuable experience if I'd taken pictures for the school newspaper.

________ 8. Kim's parents nagged her so hard about practicing the piano that they finally ___(e)d any interest she might have had in music.

________ 9. Marie and Pierre Curie ___(e)d on important scientific experiments involving radioactivity.

________ 10. The Cord, in the 1920s, was the first car with front-wheel drive, but in those days most people considered the idea ridiculous and ___(e)d at it.

NOTE: Now check your answers to these items by turning to page 129. Going over the answers carefully will help you prepare for the next two practices, for which answers are not given.

Sentence Check 2

Using the answer lines provided, complete each item below with **two** words from the box. Use each word once.

____
________ 1–2. "Everyone gets ___(e)d at now and then," Lynn said. "You just have to be ___ enough to bounce back after a facetious° remark."

____
________ 3–4. Many people who ___(e)d Dr. Martin Luther King, Jr., were ___ when he was killed, but then courageously vowed to carry on his work.

____
________ 5–6. Even though their knowledge of carpentry was only ___, the boys ___(e)d on building a treasure chest.

______________ ______________ 7–8. Being illiterate until the age of 20 didn't ___ George Washington Carver's spirit. He went on to become a great botanist—and a ___ about using peanuts, from which he made such products as ink, shampoo, and linoleum.

______________ ______________ 9–10. At the time of the American Revolution, many people viewed those who ___(e)d the rebellion as troublemakers. In ___, however, we view them as heroes.

Final Check: *Hardly a Loser*

Here is a final opportunity for you to strengthen your knowledge of the ten words. First read the following selection carefully. Then fill in each blank with a word from the box at the top of the previous page. (Context clues will help you figure out which word goes in which blank.) Use each word once.

Tom seemed to be a loser born into a long line of losers. His great-grandfather, condemned to death during the Revolutionary War for siding with the British, had fled to Canada. Tom's father, wanted for arrest after he helped (1)______________ a plot to overthrow the Canadian government, had fled back to the United States.

Tom never received even the most (2)______________ formal education. During his mere three months of schooling, he stayed at the bottom of his class. The teacher (3)______________(e)d at him, telling him that he was hopelessly stupid.

© Universal Images Group North America LLC/Alamy

Tom's first job, selling papers and candy on a train, ended when he accidentally set the baggage car on fire. His second, as a telegraph operator, ended when he was caught sleeping on the job. At 22, he was jobless, penniless, and living in a cellar. Obviously, Tom's youth had not provided the optimum° foundation for success.

Tom, however, didn't allow his situation to be a detriment° or to (4)______________ his hopes. Instead of becoming (5)______________, he was (6)______________ enough to recover from his misfortunes and find another job. He managed, in fact, to save enough money to open a workshop, where he (7)______________(e)d with an electrical engineer in designing and then selling machines. A (8)______________ when it came to solving mechanical puzzles, Tom worked nearly nonstop, sleeping only about four hours each night.

By the time he was in his 80s, Tom was credited with over a thousand inventions, including the phonograph, light bulb, and motion picture camera. He was also very famous—so much so that he was (9)______________(e)d nationwide as the greatest living American.

In (10)______________, Thomas Alva Edison wasn't such a loser after all.

Scores Sentence Check 2 ________% Final Check ________%

Enter your scores above and in the **Vocabulary Performance Chart** on the inside back cover of the book.

ambiguous	inane
dissident	juxtapose
embellish	lethargy
fritter	sporadic
inadvertent	subsidize

Ten Words in Context

In the space provided, write the letter of the meaning closest to that of each **boldfaced** word. Use the context of the sentences to help you figure out each word's meaning.

1 ambiguous
(ăm-bĭg′yo͞o-əs)
-adjective

- The portrait known as the "Mona Lisa" is famous for the woman's **ambiguous** expression. Is she smiling or not?
- Omar left an **ambiguous** message on my answering machine: "Meet me at twelve o'clock." I couldn't tell whether he meant noon or midnight.

__ *Ambiguous* means A. unclear. B. unintentional. C. unpleasant.

2 dissident
(dĭs′ə-dənt)
-noun

- It's important to remember that America's Founding Fathers, like Washington and Jefferson, were actually **dissidents** who rose up against their British rulers.
- In a dictatorship, **dissidents** are not tolerated. People who speak out against the government may be imprisoned or even executed.

__ *Dissident* means A. a rebel. B. a dishonest person. C. a foolish person.

3 embellish
(ĕm-bĕl′ĭsh)
-verb

- Lauren **embellished** the door of her room with postcards from her friends and photos of her cats.
- The cover of the biology textbook was **embellished** with a pattern of colorful seashells.

__ *Embellish* means A. to hide. B. to decorate. C. to damage.

4 fritter
(frĭt′ər)
-verb

- I thought my little sister would **fritter** away her entire allowance on M&M's, but instead of wasting her money, she put it in her piggy bank.
- Vince **fritters** away both his time and his money playing game after game in video arcades.

__ *Fritter away* means A. to earn. B. to count. C. to waste.

5 inadvertent
(ĭn′ăd-vûr′tnt)
-adjective

- Alexander Fleming's discovery of penicillin was **inadvertent**. He forgot to cover a dish of bacteria, and some mold got into it. The next day, Fleming found that the mold had killed the bacteria.
- The final draft of Nancy's paper was shorter than the previous version, but this was **inadvertent**. She had accidentally deleted an entire page without realizing it.

__ *Inadvertent* means A. not required. B. not finished. C. not intended.

6 inane
(ĭn-ān′)
-adjective

- The conversation at the party was **inane**, consisting mainly of foolish comments about whose clothes were the most "awesome."
- Television programming is often so **inane** that TV has been described as "bubble gum for the mind."

__ *Inane* means A. silly. B. interesting. C. shocking.

7 juxtapose
(jŭks′tə-pōz′)
-verb

- The photograph dramatically **juxtaposed** white birch trees and a dark gray sky.
- Dottie spread her new dress out on her bed and then **juxtaposed** all her scarves and jackets to it to see which combination would look best.

__ *Juxtapose* means A. to cover up. B. to put side by side. C. to replace.

8 lethargy
(lĕth′ər-jē)
-noun

- Although Wendy seemed to recover from the flu, her **lethargy** persisted. She felt exhausted for weeks.
- With the hot weather, **lethargy** descended upon the class. The students had trouble staying awake, and even the instructor gazed dreamily out the window.

__ *Lethargy* means A. weariness. B. hopelessness. C. foolishness.

9 sporadic
(spə-răd′ĭk)
-adjective

- It rained continuously until noon. After that, there were only **sporadic** showers.
- Dave makes **sporadic** attempts to give up smoking, but his occasional efforts have been halfhearted.

__ *Sporadic* means A. steady. B. irregular. C. long.

10 subsidize
(sŭb′sə-dīz)
-verb

- During college, many students are **subsidized** by their parents, while others rely on grants or loans.
- Public television is **subsidized** by various grants and by individual and community donations.

__ *Subsidize* means A. to pay for. B. to advertise. C. to criticize.

Matching Words with Definitions

Following are definitions of the ten words. Clearly write or print each word next to its definition. The sentences above and on the previous page will help you decide on the meaning of each word.

1. ____________________ To place close together, especially in order to compare or contrast
2. ____________________ A great lack of energy; inactivity due to laziness; sluggishness
3. ____________________ Able to be interpreted in more than one way; not clear
4. ____________________ Without sense or meaning; foolish
5. ____________________ A person opposed to established ideas or beliefs, especially in politics or religion
6. ____________________ To decorate; beautify by adding details
7. ____________________ To support financially; provide a grant or contribution
8. ____________________ To spend or waste a little at a time
9. ____________________ Unintentional; accidental
10. ____________________ Happening now and then; occasional

CAUTION: Do not go any further until you are sure the above answers are correct. Then you can use the definitions to help you in the following practices. Your goal is eventually to know the words well enough so that you don't need to check the definitions at all.

Sentence Check 1

Using the answer line provided, complete each item below with the correct word from the box. Use each word once.

A. **ambiguous**	B. **dissident**	C. **embellish**	D. **fritter**	E. **inadvertent**
F. **inane**	G. **juxtapose**	H. **lethargy**	I. **sporadic**	J. **subsidize**

_______________ 1. Tracy has learned the hard way not to ___ away her time and affection on friends who don't really care about her.

_______________ 2. My recent trip to Newark was ___. I wanted to go to New York City, but I got on the wrong train.

_______________ 3. A research grant will ___ Belinda's study of common fears among the elderly.

_______________ 4. I get news of Darren only now and then, in ___ letters from him or his mother.

_______________ 5. Instead of refreshing me, an afternoon nap only deepens my ___; I wake up even sleepier than I was before.

_______________ 6. Keisha cancelled her Facebook account. To her, it was an ___ stream of unwanted ads, fake news, and pointless pet videos.

_______________ 7. Checking a job applicant's references, the personnel manager was puzzled by one ___ comment: "You will be lucky if you can get her to work for you."

_______________ 8. When student ___s led a protest against China's communist leaders in 1989, some students were killed by government troops.

_______________ 9. In plays and movies, good and evil characters are often ___(e)d. This contrast makes the good ones seem even better and the bad ones seem even worse.

_______________ 10. My little brother has ___(e)d his bedroom ceiling with stars arranged like several of the constellations.

NOTE: Now check your answers to these items by turning to page 129. Going over the answers carefully will help you prepare for the next two practices, for which answers are not given.

Sentence Check 2

Using the answer lines provided, complete each item below with **two** words from the box. Use each word once.

____
_______________ 1–2. Local businesses ___(e)d our club's Christmas party for the homeless, so we were able to afford a special meal as well as decorations to ___ the room.

____
_______________ 3–4. On the cover of the news magazine, two pictures were ___(e)d: those of a young ___ and the elderly ruler he was opposing.

____
_______________ 5–6. "Spring fever" isn't really a detriment° to health, but it often includes ___: people just want to sleep. Also, attention to work is interrupted off and on by a(n) ___ need to daydream.

________ ________ 7–8. It's common for a TV show's season to end with a(n) ___ final episode; for example, viewers don't know if a key character is killed or survives a serious accident. This is definitely not ___ or accidental. The show's producers want to keep us guessing so we'll tune in again next season.

________ ________ 9–10. Why do you want to ___ away your money week after week on tickets for silly movies that all the critics agree are ___?

Final Check: *Grandfather at the Art Museum*

Here is a final opportunity for you to strengthen your knowledge of the ten words. First read the following selection carefully. Then fill in each blank with a word from the box at the top of the previous page. (Context clues will help you figure out which word goes in which blank.) Use each word once.

Last Saturday, my grandfather and I spent some time in the modern section of an art museum. Our visit was completely (1)________________. We'd come to see a show of nature photographs and wandered into the wrong room. Instead of leaving, Grandfather just stood there, staring at the paintings. His idea of worthwhile art is the soft-focus photography on greeting cards, and here was an exhibit of angry paintings by political (2)________________s.

In one painting, an empty plate and a plate that was piled high with food had been (3)________________(e)d on a table; the tablecloth was an American flag. Around this painting was an ornate golden frame (4)________________(e)d with tiny plastic models of hot dogs, apple pies, and other typical American foods. There was nothing (5)________________ about the message—it was crystal-clear. The artist was saying that some people in this country don't have enough to eat. After a few moments of stunned silence, my grandfather jolted the sleepy-looking guard out of his (6)________________ by shouting, "Garbage! What is this garbage?"

When we learned that two major corporations had collaborated° to (7)________________ this exhibit and even owned some of the art works, Grandfather was outraged. "How dare they (8)________________ away their money on one piece of unpatriotic trash after another while people are starving?" I started to say that the painting itself was a protest against starvation, but Grandfather just scoffed° at me. "Don't be (9)________________," he said, squelching° my attempt to explain the painting. "Let's get out of here." So we did.

On the way home, Grandfather stared out the car window. He was silent except for (10)________________ sputterings of "Garbage!" and "Incredible!"

Scores Sentence Check 2 ________% Final Check ________%

Enter your scores above and in the **Vocabulary Performance Chart** on the inside back cover of the book.

berate	**maudlin**
estrange	**regress**
euphoric	**relinquish**
impetuous	**ubiquitous**
infallible	**zenith**

Ten Words in Context

In the space provided, write the letter of the meaning closest to that of each **boldfaced** word. Use the context of the sentences to help you figure out each word's meaning.

1 berate (bĭ-rāt′) *-verb*

- Nick's mother often **berates** him. And when she isn't yelling at him, she ignores him.
- Vanessa can accept reasonable criticism, but she was upset when her boss **berated** her loudly in front of everyone else in the office.

__ *Berate* means A. to disappoint. B. to neglect. C. to scold angrily.

2 estrange (ĕ-strānj′) *-verb*

- My cousin's recent moodiness has **estranged** some of his old friends.
- After his divorce, Gavin didn't want to **estrange** his children, so he called and visited them often.

__ *Estrange* means A. to frighten. B. to drive away. C. to dislike.

3 euphoric (yo͞o-fôr′ĭk) *-adjective*

- I was **euphoric** when I received my grades. To my amazement and joy, they were all A's and B's.
- Jamil is **euphoric** today, and it's easy to see why he's in such high spirits. He just earned his black belt in judo last night, after years of study.

__ *Euphoric* means A. very happy. B. boastful. C. sentimental.

4 impetuous (ĭm-pĕch′o͞o-əs) *-adjective*

- Whenever I make an **impetuous** purchase, I end up being dissatisfied: the shoes aren't comfortable, the shirt is the wrong color, the jacket costs too much. From now on, I intend to think more carefully before I buy.
- Children tend to be **impetuous** and often don't think about the consequences of their actions. For instance, they'll throw snowballs at passing cars without worrying about possibly causing an accident.

__ *Impetuous* means A. impulsive. B. considerate. C. imaginative.

5 infallible (ĭn-făl′ə-bəl) *-adjective*

- Computers aren't **infallible**. If you put the wrong data into a computer, you'll get wrong answers.
- A facetious° sign over my sister's desk reads, "I'm **infallible**. I never make misteaks."

__ *Infallible* means A. perfect. B. imperfect. C. everywhere.

6 maudlin (môd′lĭn) *-adjective*

- The verses in greeting cards are often far too sentimental. I prefer humor to such **maudlin** messages.
- The **maudlin** movie was about a brave little orphan and his sad-eyed puppy. Everyone in the theater had tears in their eyes when the film ended.

__ *Maudlin* means A. short. B. comical. C. overly emotional.

7 regress (rĭ-grĕs′) *-verb*

- When his baby sister was born, seven-year-old Jeremy **regressed** for a while and began sucking his thumb again.
- Adolescents under stress sometimes **regress** to childish ways: dependency, temper tantrums, and silliness.

___ *Regress* means A. to go backward. B. to reach a high point. C. to act hastily.

8 relinquish (rĭ-lĭng′kwĭsh) *-verb*

- No beer is allowed in the "family area" of the stadium, so fans must **relinquish** their six-packs at the gate before they take their seats.
- Donna had to **relinquish** her share in the beach house because she couldn't afford it anymore.

___ *Relinquish* means A. to buy. B. to give up. C. to enjoy.

9 ubiquitous (yo͞o-bĭk′wə-təs) *-adjective*

- Mites are **ubiquitous**. They live on top of Mt. Everest, in the depths of the ocean, at the South Pole, and even around the roots of your hairs.
- We postponed our plan to drive home on Sunday because a dense fog was **ubiquitous**. It covered the entire town.

___ *Ubiquitous* means A. scarce. B. newly discovered. C. found everywhere.

10 zenith (zē′nĭth) *-noun*

- Florence reached the **zenith** of her career when she became president of Ace Products.
- At age 50, my uncle is afraid that he has already passed the **zenith** of his life; but at age 52, my father thinks the best is yet to come.

___ *Zenith* means A. an end. B. an earlier condition. C. the highest point.

Matching Words with Definitions

Following are definitions of the ten words. Clearly write or print each word next to its definition. The sentences above and on the previous page will help you decide on the meaning of each word.

1. ____________________ To surrender (something); give (something) up
2. ____________________ Done or acting in a hurry, with little thought; impulsive
3. ____________________ Tearfully sentimental; overly emotional
4. ____________________ To criticize or scold harshly
5. ____________________ Existing or seeming to exist everywhere at the same time
6. ____________________ The highest point or condition; peak
7. ____________________ To make unsympathetic or unfriendly; alienate
8. ____________________ Not capable of error or failure; unable to make a mistake
9. ____________________ Overjoyed; having an intense feeling of well-being
10. ____________________ To return to an earlier, generally worse, condition or behavior

CAUTION: Do not go any further until you are sure the above answers are correct. Then you can use the definitions to help you in the following practices. Your goal is eventually to know the words well enough so that you don't need to check the definitions at all.

Sentence Check 1

Using the answer line provided, complete each item below with the correct word from the box. Use each word once.

A. berate	B. estrange	C. euphoric	D. impetuous	E. infallible
F. maudlin	G. regress	H. relinquish	I. ubiquitous	J. zenith

_______________ 1. Kay used to be friendly, but since her promotion, she has become so cold that she has ___(e)d former coworkers.

_______________ 2. When Dad lost his job, he had to ___ his identification card, his employee parking permit, and the key to his desk.

_______________ 3. Mei Lin was ___ when the college that was her first choice accepted her.

_______________ 4. To many people, Mozart's works represent the ___ of eighteenth-century music.

_______________ 5. People in bombed-out, war-torn cities are sometimes forced to ___ to more primitive ways of life.

_______________ 6. Joyce isn't usually ___, but last week she had a sudden urge to try out her nephew's skateboard. Everyone in the office has already signed the cast on her broken wrist.

_______________ 7. Uncle George becomes ___ when he talks about his dear old mother in Greece. Tears also come to the eyes of all who listen.

_______________ 8. In our neighborhood, litter is ___—the sidewalks are ankle-deep in trash. We need a cleanup campaign.

_______________ 9. "I know I was late," Liz said, "but you could have pointed it out quietly. You didn't have to ___ me."

_______________ 10. "I don't expect you to be ___," the boss said, "but I don't want you to make the same mistakes over and over."

NOTE: Now check your answers to these items by turning to page 129. Going over the answers carefully will help you prepare for the next two practices, for which answers are not given.

Sentence Check 2

Using the answer lines provided, complete each item below with **two** words from the box. Use each word once.

____
_______________ 1–2. Since my father died, reminders of him seem ___. I know I'm being ___, but everywhere I look, I see something that makes me cry.

____
_______________ 3–4. I'm trying to be less ___, but I still sometimes act on impulse. Later, in retrospect°, I always ___ myself for not using better judgment.

____
_______________ 5–6. If people were ___, we could ___ our pencil erasers and the "delete" key.

______ ______ 7–8. Our neighborhood basketball team reached its ___ when it won the citywide championship. The local businesses that had subsidized° the team were delighted, and the players themselves were ___.

______ ______ 9–10. Patrick ___(e)d his wife when he wasted their money on gambling and ostentatious° clothes. Since their separation, their young daughter has ___(e)d to infantile behavior.

Final Check: *An Artist Named Vincent*

Here is a final opportunity for you to strengthen your knowledge of the ten words. First read the following selection carefully. Then fill in each blank with a word from the box at the top of the previous page. (Context clues will help you figure out which word goes in which blank.) Use each word once.

The Dutch artist Vincent Van Gogh (commonly pronounced *van-GO*) is world-famous for his paintings, which sell for jaw-dropping sums—many millions of dollars. Posters of his work, most famously "The Starry Night," are (1)________________; they can be found in any poster shop or website. But poor Van Gogh did not enjoy fame and fortune during his lifetime. Indeed, he sold only one painting before he died in 1890.

© Everett-Art/shutterstock.com

Van Gogh's lack of success is tied to the fact that he was almost certainly mentally ill. He was known for having very extreme mood swings. For several weeks he would be (2)________________, convinced that he was the greatest of painters and on the verge of success. During the (3)________________ of those periods, he believed he was (4)________________, unable to consider that he might be wrong about anything. He would paint constantly, rarely stopping to eat or sleep. He acted in (5)________________ ways, such as buying great quantities of books and art supplies that he could not afford. He would (6)________________ his friends by borrowing money from them that he would never repay. Instead of apologizing for his debt, he would (7)________________ those same friends for not believing in his talent.

Then, just as suddenly, Van Gogh would collapse. He would become (8)________________ and terribly depressed, unable to do anything but cry and sleep. This cycle continued; for a while he would seem normal, then intensely happy and gregarious°, and then he would (9)________________ into a very dark mental state, becoming despondent°. Amidst a final bout with depression, he (10)________________(e)d his hope of ever getting better and committed suicide.

It is tragic that Van Gogh lived at a time when mental illness was poorly understood. Today, it is very likely that treatment and medications could have allowed him to live a longer and far happier life.

Scores Sentence Check 2 ________% Final Check ________%

Enter your scores above and in the **Vocabulary Performance Chart** on the inside back cover of the book.

equivocate
fortuitous
impeccable
liaison
predisposed
propensity
reprehensible
sham
solace
solicitous

Ten Words in Context

In the space provided, write the letter of the meaning closest to that of each **boldfaced** word. Use the context of the sentences to help you figure out each word's meaning.

1 equivocate
(ē-kwĭv′ə-kāt′)
-verb

- Bob can't get his boss to say whether or not he intends to give him a raise. When Bob asks him, he **equivocates**, saying, "You've been doing good work, Bob."
- Lonnell doesn't want to come right out and tell Tiffany he doesn't love her. If she asks, he **equivocates** by telling her something like "You know how I feel."

__ *Equivocate* means A. to be blunt. B. to be unclear. C. to deny.

2 fortuitous
(fôr-to͞o′ə-təs)
-adjective

- How **fortuitous** that I found a phone charger on the sidewalk when I had just lost mine!
- It was strictly **fortuitous** that Vince found his missing class notes. They happened to drop out of his textbook when it fell to the floor.

__ *Fortuitous* means A. accidental. B. predictable. C. overdue.

3 impeccable
(ĭm-pĕk′ə-bəl)
-adjective

- My aunt always looks stylish but never overdressed. Her taste in clothes is **impeccable**.
- When she auditioned for the play, Julie gave an **impeccable** performance. She read the lines perfectly and got the part.

__ *Impeccable* means A. flawless. B. deceptive. C. faulty.

4 liaison
(lē-ā′zŏn′)
-noun

- The president of the Student Council acts as a **liaison** between the students and the administration.
- Because she is bilingual, Elena often serves as a **liaison** between the Spanish- and English-speaking personnel in her office.

__ *Liaison* means A. a follower. B. a caregiver. C. a link.

5 predisposed
(prē′dĭs-pōzd′)
-adjective

- Terry didn't want to move in the first place, so she was **predisposed** to hate the new apartment.
- Angel's mother and grandmother were tall and very athletic, so Angel was **predisposed** to being a good basketball player.

__ *Predisposed* means A. unlikely. B. likely. C. pretending.

6 propensity
(prə-pĕn′sĭ-tē)
-noun

- Because Ivan has a **propensity** to gain weight, he watches what he eats.
- Cheryl is aware of her **propensity** to blab, so she warns her friends not to tell her anything they wouldn't want repeated.

__ *Propensity* means A. a coincidence. B. an inclination. C. a concern.

7 reprehensible
(rĕp′rĭ-hĕn′sə-bəl)
-adjective

- The Riordans never discipline their son. No matter how **reprehensible** his behavior is, they just say, "Kids will be kids."
- The company's failure to clean up the oil spill was **reprehensible** and drew harsh criticism.

__ *Reprehensible* means A. shameful. B. misleading. C. uncertain.

8 sham
(shăm)
-noun

- Karen's apparent affection for Raul is a **sham**. He's rich, and she cares only about his money.
- When the city inspectors came, the restaurant kitchen was sparkling. However, such cleanliness was a **sham**—the place is usually filthy.

__ *Sham* means A. something false. B. something confusing. C. something accidental.

9 solace
(sŏl′ĭs)
-noun

- After a family quarrel, Tamara finds **solace** in the privacy and quiet of her own room.
- Whenever I'm upset and need **solace**, I call my friend Lisa. Talking to her always makes me feel better.

__ *Solace* means A. excitement. B. perfection. C. relief.

10 solicitous
(sə-lĭs′ĭ-təs)
-adjective

- The waiter was overly **solicitous**. He kept interrupting our conversation to ask, "Is everything all right here?"
- **Solicitous** toward her elderly neighbor, Marie calls every day to see how he is feeling and if he needs anything.

__ *Solicitous* means A. distant. B. attentive. C. patient.

Matching Words with Definitions

Following are definitions of the ten words. Clearly write or print each word next to its definition. The sentences above and on the previous page will help you decide on the meaning of each word.

1. ________________ A natural preference or tendency
2. ________________ Deserving of blame, criticism, or disapproval
3. ________________ Happening by chance, by accident, or at random; lucky
4. ________________ Comfort in sorrow or misfortune; consolation
5. ________________ A person who serves as a connection between individuals or groups; a go-between
6. ________________ To be deliberately vague in order to mislead
7. ________________ Faultless; perfect
8. ________________ Showing or expressing concern, care, or attention
9. ________________ Tending toward or open to something beforehand
10. ________________ A pretense or counterfeit; something meant to deceive

CAUTION: Do not go any further until you are sure the above answers are correct. Then you can use the definitions to help you in the following practices. Your goal is eventually to know the words well enough so that you don't need to check the definitions at all.

Sentence Check 1

Using the answer line provided, complete each item below with the correct word from the box. Use each word once.

A. **equivocate**	B. **fortuitous**	C. **impeccable**	D. **liaison**	E. **predisposed**
F. **propensity**	G. **reprehensible**	H. **sham**	I. **solace**	J. **solicitous**

________ 1. Many people consider child abuse such a(n) ___ crime that they think the penalties should be as harsh as possible.

________ 2. My brother and I are both grown up, but Mom is still ___ about our health. She says, "You'll always be my babies."

________ 3. The boss is in a rotten mood today, so he's not ___ to tolerate any mistakes.

________ 4. Jan writes at least three drafts of every paper so that the final result will be ___. She wants each assignment she turns in to be perfect.

________ 5. When my grandmother died, I found ___ in the thought that she had lived a long, happy life.

________ 6. The job candidate ___(e)d when he said he'd been "working out West." Actually, he'd been a ski bum for three years.

________ 7. For several months, Olive acted as a ___ between her divorced parents, but she finally insisted that they deal with each other directly.

________ 8. Unexpectedly, I ran into a former neighbor who had just started her own business. The ___ meeting led to a summer job offer for me.

________ 9. It's hard to believe that Stacy, with her ___ for flashy clothes and expensive lifestyle, has become a social worker.

________ 10. The "going-out-of-business" sale was a ___. A year later, the store was still open.

NOTE: Now check your answers to these items by turning to page 129. Going over the answers carefully will help you prepare for the next two practices, for which answers are not given.

Sentence Check 2

Using the answer lines provided, complete each item below with **two** words from the box. Use each word once.

____
________ 1–2. Even before I met my father's nurse, I was ___ to like her, because I had heard how ___ she was toward him.

____
________ 3–4. The woman wasn't permitted to visit her husband, a political prisoner, so it gave her some ___ to have a minister act as a ___ between them.

____
________ 5–6. When Shirley said she was annoyed by Len's ___ to use her favorite coffee mug, he ___(e)d by making an ambiguous° statement: "I promise you'll never catch me using it again."

_______________ 7–8. The artist was in the illicit° business of making copies of paintings, then selling them as originals. His work was so ___ that even museum owners didn't realize the paintings were ___s.
____

_______________ 9–10. It was strictly ___ that no one was killed when the chemical plant exploded. The explosion, however, was no matter of chance, but the result of ___ carelessness on the part of an employee.
____

Final Check: *A Phony Friend*

Here is a final opportunity for you to strengthen your knowledge of the ten words. First read the following selection carefully. Then fill in each blank with a word from the box at the top of the previous page. (Context clues will help you figure out which word goes in which blank.) Use each word once.

When my grandfather, Henry Altman, died, he left me a large sum of money. This was very surprising because he and my father had become estranged° years before, after a quarrel, and the old man had never even seen me. I was sad that he had died before we could meet.

Soon after the news of my inheritance, a young man named Seth showed up to offer me his sympathy. Seth said he had been a friend of my grandfather's and that when the old man had become ill, he'd asked Seth to act as a (1)_______________ between himself and the granddaughter he'd never met. "It's too late for Henry," said Seth, "but I think he'd want me to offer you my friendship. In his later years, he regretted his earlier (2)_______________ to quarrel with his family."

© Karen Roach/123rf.com

Believing that Seth had been my grandfather's friend made me (3)_______________ to like him, and it gave me (4)_______________ to speak to someone who had known my grandfather. Still, I was puzzled because Seth wasn't able to give me much information. For example, when I asked some questions about Grandfather's second wife, Seth seemed to (5)_______________, saying, "All I can say is that she was quite a woman." On the other hand, Seth appeared genuinely (6)_______________ about my welfare, and his manners were (7)_______________. I had never met anyone so perfectly polite.

I really didn't know what to make of him until, one day, I had a(n) (8)_______________ meeting with an old school friend I hadn't seen in years. When I told her about Seth and showed her his online profile picture, my friend looked startled and said, "I know that guy. He's a phony, a crook—a complete (9) _______________. He's after the money, and I bet he never even knew your grandfather."

When I checked, my friend's story was supported by reports of how Seth had tricked several other women out of their inheritances. The next time he called, I told him I knew about his (10)_______________ behavior and would notify the police if he ever tried to contact me again.

Scores Sentence Check 2 _______% Final Check _______%

Enter your scores above and in the **Vocabulary Performance Chart** on the inside back cover of the book.

UNIT ONE: Review

The box at the right lists twenty-five words from Unit One. Using the clues at the bottom of the page, fill in these words to complete the puzzle that follows.

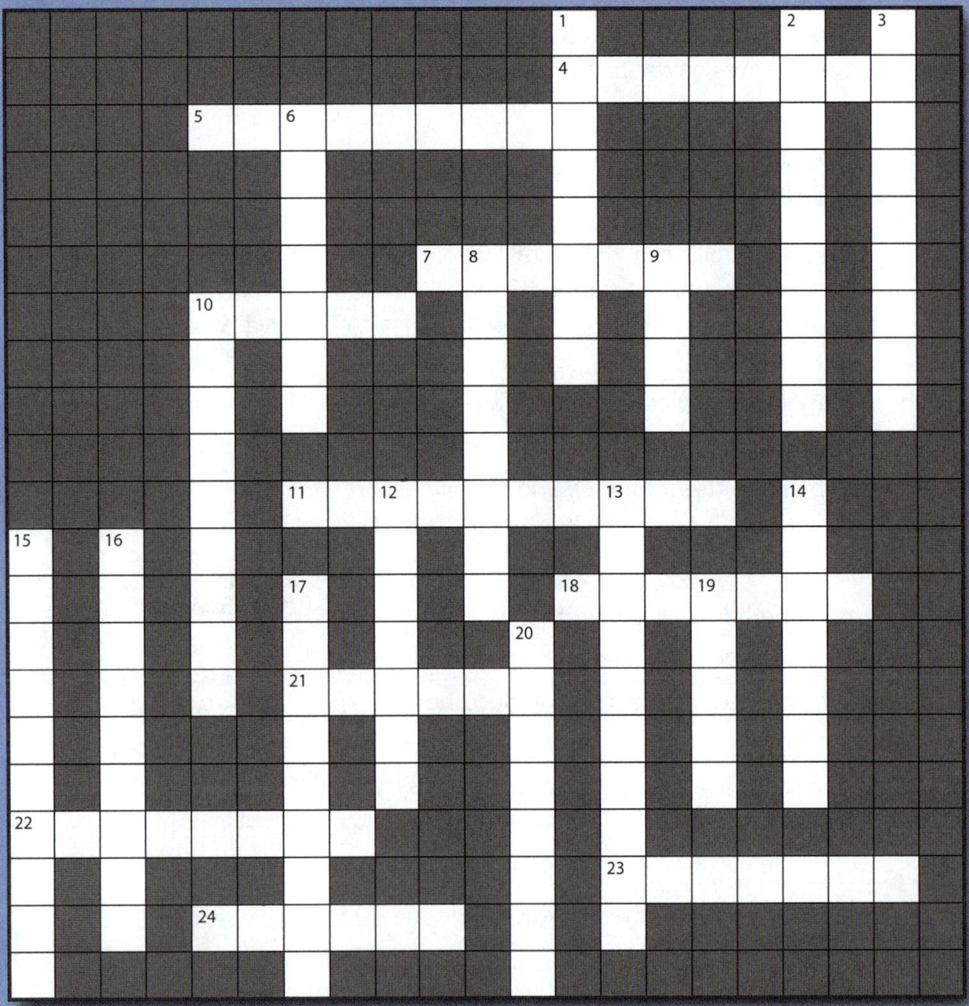

detriment
discretion
dissident
estrange
euphoric
impeccable
inane
instigate
lethargy
liaison
maudlin
optimum
propensity
regress
resilient
scoff
sensory
sham
solace
sporadic
squelch
subsidize
venerate
vicarious
zenith

ACROSS

4. To make unsympathetic or unfriendly; alienate
5. A person opposed to established ideas or beliefs
7. To return to an earlier, generally worse, condition or behavior
10. To make fun of; mock
11. Good judgment or tact in actions or speaking
18. Best possible; most favorable
21. Comfort for sorrow or misfortune; consolation
22. Happening now and then; occasional
23. A person who serves as a connection between individuals or groups
24. The highest point; peak

DOWN

1. A great lack of energy
2. To bring about by moving others to action; stir up
3. Something that causes damage, harm, or loss
6. Having to do with seeing, hearing, feeling, tasting, or smelling
8. Overjoyed; having an intense feeling of well-being
9. A pretense or counterfeit; something meant to deceive
10. To support financially
12. To silence or suppress; crush
13. Faultless; perfect
14. Tearfully sentimental; over-emotional
15. A natural preference or tendency
16. Experienced through the imagination
17. Able to recover quickly from harm, illness, or misfortune
19. Without sense or meaning; foolish
20. To respect deeply; revere

UNIT ONE: Test 1

PART A

Choose the word that best completes each item and write it in the space provided.

______________ 1. The invitation we sent my parents to attend a friend's birthday party was a ___. We were actually giving a surprise party in honor of their anniversary.

A. detriment B. propensity C. solace D. sham

______________ 2. Grandfather was known for being ___. Once he spent twenty-five cents for the trolley in order to go back to a store and return the extra nickel that he had received in change.

A. ambiguous B. scrupulous C. vicarious D. reprehensible

______________ 3. If Bart's parents leave him alone with his sister for even thirty seconds, he ___ a fight with her.

A. subsidizes B. collaborates C. instigates D. juxtaposes

______________ 4. When I asked my father if he liked my new dress, he ___, saying, "That green is a terrific color."

A. equivocated B. venerated C. relinquished D. collaborated

______________ 5. Our brains interpret our ___ impressions for us. For instance, the images of things we look at must go to the brain so we can actually "see" them.

A. inadvertent B. scrupulous C. sensory D. resilient

______________ 6. I thought the handyman was being ___ when he said he had to cut a bigger hole in my wall in order to fix the little hole, but that's exactly what he did.

A. dexterous B. facetious C. ubiquitous D. maudlin

______________ 7. Jaime's shyness may be a ___ to an acting career, in which it helps to be aggressive.

A. propensity B. dissident C. zenith D. detriment

______________ 8. I tried to ___ the laugh rising in my throat, but seeing the boss looking all over his desk for the glasses he had pushed up on his head was too funny.

A. squelch B. venerate C. berate D. scoff

______________ 9. When he's caught in a tight spot, Peter has an unfortunate ___ to lie. As a result, few people trust him anymore.

A. retrospect B. propensity C. zenith D. sham

______________ 10. Many movie fans ___ *The Godfather* and consider it the best film ever made.

A. berate B. venerate C. juxtapose D. fritter

(Continues on next page)

PART B

On the answer line, write the letter of the choice that best completes each item.

____ 11. Gene **embellished** his car by
- A. adding fancy hubcaps and a two-tone paint job.
- B. changing the oil at least every three thousand miles.
- C. not getting rid of soda cans and fast-food wrappers.
- D. never having it serviced and letting the engine burn out.

____ 12. Keith is known for being **impetuous**. Last week, he
- A. signed up to become a foster parent after thinking about it for several months.
- B. received the "Most Dependable Employee" award at his workplace.
- C. suddenly decided to drive across six states to visit a childhood friend, without even checking to see if the friend was at home.
- D. refused to lend his mother the money she needed to have some emergency dental work done.

____ 13. Valerie received an unexpected inheritance of $1000. She **frittered** it away by
- A. giving it to her parents to pay household bills.
- B. making a down payment on a car.
- C. spending it on clothing and lottery tickets.
- D. putting it into her college savings fund.

____ 14. A **resilient** person who gets the flu
- A. will probably need a long time to recover.
- B. is soon able to resume her normal activities.
- C. complains endlessly about her misfortune.
- D. becomes afraid she'll catch something else.

____ 15. Some people become downright **maudlin** at weddings. For instance, when my sister got married, Uncle Arthur
- A. refused to kiss the bride.
- B. hugged her and sobbed, "You're leaving us!"
- C. seemed quiet and depressed.
- D. laughed, told jokes, and danced up a storm.

____ 16. Your brother has just announced that he plans to be president someday. You **scoff** at him, saying,
- A. "Right. And I'm going to be the Queen of England."
- B. "That'd be pretty hard, but I bet you could do it."
- C. "Tell me why you are interested in doing that."
- D. "It's cool that you're aiming so high."

____ 17. An essay called "How To **Estrange** Your Friends" might suggest
- A. inviting friends to your house to watch videos, eat pizza, and hang out.
- B. offering to teach friends a sport or skill that you're good at.
- C. noticing when friends are feeling depressed and sending them a card or a little gift.
- D. borrowing friends' money and not repaying it.

____ 18. You would most likely become **despondent** if
- A. it's a beautiful sunny day, your work is all done, and you've got money in your pocket.
- B. your boss has asked to see you, and you don't know if you're going to be fired or promoted.
- C. the restaurant you went to for lunch was out of your favorite kind of pie.
- D. your best friend is moving away, you've lost your job, and your car has broken down.

____ 19. At a party, a **gregarious** person is likely to
- A. be part of a lively group of people.
- B. leave early.
- C. sit and talk with just one person all evening.
- D. begin an argument over something silly.

____ 20. You can consider an event in **retrospect** only
- A. after the event has occurred.
- B. before the event happens.
- C. if the event is a happy one.
- D. while the event is actually happening.

Score (Number correct) ________ x 5 = ________%

Enter your score above and in the **Vocabulary Performance Chart** on the inside back cover of the book.

UNIT ONE: Test 2

PART A

Complete each item with a word from the box. Use each word once.

A. **ambiguous**	B. **euphoric**	C. **infallible**	D. **juxtapose**	E. **lethargy**
F. **predisposed**	G. **regress**	H. **relinquish**	I. **solace**	J. **subsidize**
K. **vicarious**	L. **zealot**	M. **zenith**		

________________ 1. The Bradleys won't go on vacation until their new puppy is fully trained. They're afraid that if he stays at the kennel for a week, he will ___ and start ruining the rugs again.

________________ 2. After her first husband died from alcohol-related causes, Carrie Nation became an anti-drinking ___. In the early 1990s, she traveled around the country campaigning against alcohol and destroying dozens of saloons with a hatchet.

________________ 3. After a big picnic meal in the warm sun, a(n) ___ came over me, so I took a nap under a maple tree.

________________ 4. "If you don't maintain a B average," said the coach, "you ___ your right to be on this team."

________________ 5. Literature and drama allow us to experience problems in a(n) ___ way, giving us painless opportunities to shape our real-life views.

________________ 6. Public TV stations hold fund drives to encourage their viewers to help ___ the costs of their programs.

________________ 7. Kaylin's family was ___ when she arrived home, alive and well, three hours late. She had missed her plane, the one that had crashed.

________________ 8. Jason sounds so sure of himself that he gives people the impression he is ___. But he makes mistakes too, just like the rest of us.

________________ 9. Because his father and grandfather both had heart disease, my cousin worries that he may be ___ to the same disorder.

________________ 10. When their young daughter died last year, the Bakers found ___ with a support group of other parents who had also lost a child.

________________ 11. When my older sister asked whether she and her seven kids could visit us for a week, my mother's response was so ___ that I'm not sure if she said yes or no.

________________ 12. Some people who reach the ___ of their careers find that "it's lonely at the top."

________________ 13. To provide contrast, the photographer ___(e)d the men in their dark suits and the women in their pale dresses.

(Continues on next page)

PART B

Write **C** if the italicized word is used **correctly**. Write **I** if the word is used **incorrectly**.

____ 14. I'm not surprised that Lucy is protesting the governor's new welfare policy. She is known for being a *dissident*.

____ 15. The hotel offers the *optimum* in accommodations. The only guests who ever return there (with friends and relations) are the roaches.

____ 16. Theo's behavior toward his sister is *reprehensible*. He shouldn't be allowed to mistreat her so.

____ 17. In wood shop, we had to learn *rudimentary* skills before we could actually make something.

____ 18. My aunt and uncle are rich but *ostentatious*. Judging by their modest possessions, you'd never know how much money they really have.

____ 19. Earth happens to be a place where oxygen is *ubiquitous*, making the planet suitable for many forms of life.

____ 20. Use *discretion* about where to consult with your doctor. If you run into him or her at church or the supermarket, it's not appropriate to ask about your warts or athlete's foot.

____ 21. Meeting my brother in the cafeteria at lunchtime was *inadvertent*. We had arranged the night before to meet for lunch.

____ 22. During my childhood, we made *sporadic* visits to my grandparents' house. Not a Sunday passed that we didn't see them.

____ 23. As a *liaison* between the hospital staff and patients' families, Jon provides information about patients' conditions in language their families can understand.

____ 24. Sally's appearance was *impeccable*. Even her fingernails were dirty.

____ 25. A tightrope walker must be both *dexterous* and unafraid of heights.

Score (Number correct) ________ x 4 = ________%

Enter your score above and in the **Vocabulary Performance Chart** on the inside back cover of the book.

UNIT ONE: Test 3

PART A: Synonyms

In the space provided, write the letter of the choice that is most nearly the **same** in meaning as the **boldfaced** word.

		A.	B.	C.	D.
____	1. **liaison**	A. tactful	B. pretender	C. connecting link	D. supporter
____	2. **solace**	A. drowsiness	B. comfort	C. friendship	D. misfortune
____	3. **subsidize**	A. support	B. order	C. beautify	D. make unfriendly
____	4. **dexterous**	A. skillful	B. faultless	C. reliable	D. joking
____	5. **sensory**	A. emotional	B. pleasing	C. logical	D. of the senses
____	6. **retrospect**	A. looking back	B. peak	C. waiting	D. prediction
____	7. **embellish**	A. ridicule	B. decorate	C. scold	D. set side by side
____	8. **predisposed**	A. early	B. lucky	C. aware	D. tending toward
____	9. **estrange**	A. give up	B. waste	C. drive away	D. puzzle
____	10. **facetious**	A. humorous	B. sad	C. careless	D. skillful
____	11. **infallible**	A. successful	B. cautious	C. endless	D. faultless
____	12. **discretion**	A. obedience	B. tact	C. imitation	D. goodwill
____	13. **collaborate**	A. decorate	B. stop	C. work together	D. start
____	14. **resilient**	A. showy	B. joyful	C. depressed	D. rapidly recovering
____	15. **juxtapose**	A. work together	B. set side by side	C. imitate	D. avoid the issue
____	16. **fortuitous**	A. accidental	B. planned	C. strong	D. witty
____	17. **impeccable**	A. impossible	B. cautious	C. flawless	D. well-informed
____	18. **dissident**	A. imitator	B. one who doubts	C. supporter	D. protester
____	19. **equivocate**	A. mock	B. become equal	C. begin	D. be purposely vague
____	20. **propensity**	A. tendency	B. talent	C. tact	D. achievement
____	21. **detriment**	A. benefit	B. harm	C. imitation	D. accident
____	22. **zealot**	A. doubter	B. sinner	C. enthusiast	D. impostor
____	23. **sporadic**	A. irregular	B. steady	C. impulsive	D. reliable
____	24. **venerate**	A. notice	B. like	C. respect	D. appreciate
____	25. **vicarious**	A. pleasant	B. difficult	C. lively	D. indirect

(Continues on next page)

PART B: Antonyms

In the space provided, write the letter of the choice that is most nearly the **opposite** in meaning to the **boldfaced** word.

____ 26. **maudlin** A. conscientious B. caring C. confident D. unemotional

____ 27. **ubiquitous** A. unlucky B. rarely found C. illegal D. moral

____ 28. **rudimentary** A. thorough B. unclear C. advanced D. immoral

____ 29. **gregarious** A. unsociable B. obedient C. evil D. unknown

____ 30. **berate** A. keep B. help C. avoid D. compliment

____ 31. **inane** A. sensible B. old C. humorous D. skillful

____ 32. **instigate** A. describe B. prevent C. leave D. waste

____ 33. **regress** A. choose B. support C. inform D. make progress

____ 34. **despondent** A. curious B. happy C. rich D. caring

____ 35. **scoff** A. investigate B. offer C. praise D. invite

____ 36. **ambiguous** A. clear B. correct C. interesting D. worthwhile

____ 37. **reprehensible** A. accidental B. educated C. praiseworthy D. famous

____ 38. **inadvertent** A. accurate B. helpful C. serious D. intentional

____ 39. **euphoric** A. unfriendly B. modest C. depressed D. curious

____ 40. **ostentatious** A. modest B. poor C. sickly D. weak

____ 41. **zenith** A. challenge B. young C. average D. bottom

____ 42. **scrupulous** A. misinformed B. dishonest C. lazy D. rich

____ 43. **relinquish** A. keep B. create C. donate D. prevent

____ 44. **solicitous** A. shy B. unconcerned C. sad D. generous

____ 45. **sham** A. advantage B. praise C. success D. an original

____ 46. **optimum** A. best B. worst C. necessary D. same

____ 47. **squelch** A. use B. ridicule C. encourage D. locate

____ 48. **lethargy** A. dullness B. liveliness C. relief D. disadvantage

____ 49. **impetuous** A. sad B. cautious C. rapid D. perfect

____ 50. **fritter** A. oppose B. respect C. support D. save

Score (Number correct) ________ x 2 = ________%

Enter your score above and in the **Vocabulary Performance Chart** on the inside back cover of the book.

UNIT ONE: Test 4

Each item below starts with a pair of words in CAPITAL LETTERS. For each item, figure out the relationship between these two words. Then decide which of the choices (A, B, C, or D) expresses a similar relationship. Write the letter of your choice on the answer line.

____ 1. AMBIGUOUS : MISUNDERSTAND ::
A. funny : laugh
B. doubtful : agree
C. boring : enjoy
D. clear : disagree

____ 2. DISSIDENT : SUPPORT ::
A. customer : pay
B. soprano : sing
C. actor : comedy
D. leader : follow

____ 3. GREGARIOUS : UNSOCIABLE ::
A. ambitious : hardworking
B. enormous : tiny
C. jealous : possessive
D. famous : rich

____ 4. OPTIMUM : GOOD ::
A. worst : bad
B. best : worse
C. careful : careless
D. high : low

____ 5. COLLABORATE : TEAMMATES ::
A. fight : pacifists
B. watch : listen
C. compete : rivals
D. bark : cats

____ 6. DESPONDENT : HOPELESS ::
A. sensible : careless
B. popular : friendless
C. generous : donation
D. fortunate : lucky

____ 7. RUDIMENTARY : JELL-O ::
A. outdated : pudding
B. advanced : wedding cake
C. expensive : donut
D. simple : French pastry

____ 8. ZEALOT : SPORTS FAN ::
A. musician : biologist
B. athlete : runner
C. scientist : wrestler
D. writer : reader

____ 9. DETRIMENT : ADVANTAGE ::
A. help : assistance
B. work : digging
C. determination : persistence
D. forgetting : remembering

____ 10. DEXTEROUS : BRAIN SURGEON ::
A. strong : weightlifter
B. young : violinist
C. honest : bank robber
D. neat : mathematician

(Continues on next page)

_____ 11. SHAM : DISGUISE ::
A. plan : blueprint
B. smile : frown
C. framework : building
D. mask : face

_____ 12. SOLICITOUS : UNCARING ::
A. sole : only
B. satisfying : displeasing
C. solar : system
D. solitary : alone

_____ 13. BERATE : NAUGHTY CHILD ::
A. comfort : lottery winner
B. congratulate : grieving widow
C. obey : prisoner
D. praise : hardworking student

_____ 14. EUPHORIC : SCHOLARSHIP WINNER ::
A. calm : bride
B. angry : puppy
C. frightened : hostage
D. surprised : instructor

_____ 15. IMPETUOUS : CAUTIOUS ::
A. passionate : unemotional
B. quiet : handsome
C. cheerful : encouraging
D. shy : timid

_____ 16. UBIQUITOUS : AIR ::
A. rare : cellular phone
B. ferocious: giraffe
C. playful : insect
D. sparkling : diamond

_____ 17. FORTUITOUS : BY CHANCE ::
A. anonymous : by name
B. blessed : unlucky
C. commonplace : familiar
D. automated : by hand

_____ 18. REPREHENSIBLE : MURDER ::
A. enjoyable : sickness
B. praiseworthy : good deed
C. impossible : fact
D. terrible : kindness

_____ 19. EMBELLISH : COLORED LIGHTS ::
A. exercise : armchair
B. destroy : dynamite
C. eat : nails
D. sign : scissors

_____ 20. INANE : SENSELESS ::
A. injured : hurt
B. pleasing : flower
C. flawed : perfect
D. audible : odorless

Score (Number correct) ________ x 5 = ________%

Enter your score above and in the **Vocabulary Performance Chart** on the inside back cover of the book.

Unit Two

Chapter 6

attrition	oblivious
circumvent	reticent
cohesive	robust
grievous	sanction
inundate	vociferous

Chapter 7

bolster	relegate
depreciate	replete
indiscriminate	sedentary
inquisitive	tenet
nebulous	terse

Chapter 8

clandestine	indigenous
contingency	liability
egocentric	prolific
exonerate	reinstate
incongruous	superfluous

Chapter 9

austere	metamorphosis
esoteric	notorious
facsimile	perfunctory
grotesque	provocative
mesmerize	travesty

Chapter 10

connoisseur	lucid
conspiracy	plight
contrite	superficially
distraught	symmetrical
germane	verbose

attrition	oblivious
circumvent	reticent
cohesive	robust
grievous	sanction
inundate	vociferous

Ten Words in Context

In the space provided, write the letter of the meaning closest to that of each **boldfaced** word. Use the context of the sentences to help you figure out each word's meaning.

1 **attrition**
(ə-trĭsh′ən)
-noun

- Sports teams are constantly looking for new talent to replace players lost through **attrition**—those who retire, quit because of injuries, and so on.
- Colleges try not to have a high rate of **attrition**. They want students to stay until graduation, rather than drop out early.

__ *Attrition* means A. an increase in numbers. B. a natural loss of individuals. C. ill health.

2 **circumvent**
(sŭr′kəm-vĕnt′)
-verb

- If we take this roundabout route, we can **circumvent** the rush-hour traffic and get home early.
- Our terrified cat **circumvents** the vacuum cleaner by sprinting around the edge of the room.

__ *Circumvent* means A. to avoid. B. to meet head-on. C. to make smaller.

3 **cohesive**
(kō-hē′sĭv)
-adjective

- For a **cohesive** pie dough, one that doesn't fall apart, be sure to add enough liquid.
- A family needs to be **cohesive**—to stay together even when stresses and strains threaten to tear it apart.

__ *Cohesive* means A. connected. B. popular. C. large.

4 **grievous**
(grēv′əs)
-adjective

- The death of a beloved pet is a **grievous** loss for a child.
- The assassination of a great leader, such as Mahatma Gandhi or Martin Luther King, Jr., often does **grievous** harm to a society.

__ *Grievous* means A. preventable. B. unavoidable. C. terrible.

5 **inundate**
(ĭn′ŭn-dāt′)
-verb

- During the heavy rains, the river overflowed and **inundated** the fields, destroying all the crops.
- After his brief announcement at the beginning of the press conference, the president was **inundated** with questions from reporters.

__ *Inundate* means A. to flood. B. to strengthen. C. to go around.

6 **oblivious**
(ə-blĭv′ē-əs)
-adjective

- The driver continued into the intersection, apparently **oblivious** to the fact that the light had turned red.
- It's easy to spot two people in love. They are the ones who, **oblivious** to everyone else present, see only each other.

__ *Oblivious to* means A. angry about. B. not noticing. C. overwhelmed by.

7 reticent
(rĕt′ĭ-sənt)
-adjective

- Lamar is very **reticent** about his first marriage; he never talks about his former wife or what led to their divorce.
- It's odd that many people who love to gossip about someone else are so **reticent** about their own lives.

__ *Reticent* means A. dishonest. B. quiet. C. unaware.

8 robust
(rō-bŭst′)
-adjective

- Once an energetic, **robust** man, Mr. Rand has been considerably weakened by illness.
- A number of weightlifters who were previously **robust** have ruined their health and vigor by taking steroids.

__ *Robust* means A. very noisy. B. sickly. C. strong and well.

9 sanction
(săngk′shən)
-verb

- By greeting the dictator with extreme courtesy and fanfare, the ambassador seemed to **sanction** his policies.
- Many people whose children attend religious schools would like the government to **sanction** the use of public funds to help pay for their education.

__ *Sanction* means A. to grant approval of. B. to criticize severely. C. to remember.

10 vociferous
(vō-sĭf′ər-əs)
-adjective

- When male loons sense that their territory is being invaded, they give **vociferous** cries of challenge.
- The principal became angry and **vociferous**, shouting at students who tried to sneak out of the fire drill.

__ *Vociferous* means A. distant. B. mild. C. loud.

Matching Words with Definitions

Following are definitions of the ten words. Clearly write or print each word next to its definition. The sentences above and on the previous page will help you decide on the meaning of each word.

1. ____________________ To authorize, allow, or approve
2. ____________________ To cover, as by flooding; overwhelm with a large number or amount
3. ____________________ To avoid by going around; to escape from, prevent, or stop through cleverness
4. ____________________ Quiet or uncommunicative; reluctant to speak out
5. ____________________ Healthy and strong; vigorous
6. ____________________ Sticking or holding together; unified
7. ____________________ Noisy; expressing feelings loudly and intensely
8. ____________________ A gradual natural decrease in number; becoming fewer in number
9. ____________________ Causing grief or pain; very serious or severe
10. ____________________ Unaware; failing to notice

CAUTION: Do not go any further until you are sure the above answers are correct. Then you can use the definitions to help you in the following practices. Your goal is eventually to know the words well enough so that you don't need to check the definitions at all.

Sentence Check 1

Using the answer line provided, complete each item below with the correct word from the box. Use each word once.

A. **attrition**	B. **circumvent**	C. **cohesive**	D. **grievous**	E. **inundate**
F. **oblivious**	G. **reticent**	H. **robust**	I. **sanction**	J. **vociferous**

_______ 1. People sometimes do odd things to ___ regulations. In New York, when saloons were illegal, one owner called his place "O'Neal's Baloon."

_______ 2. A half-hour of aerobic exercise every other day will help you stay ___.

_______ 3. In many places, the law doesn't ___ gambling—but the officials don't do much to stop it, either.

_______ 4. A quiet, polite discussion may be better than a(n) ___ argument, but some people get more satisfaction out of yelling and shouting.

_______ 5. The chatty, slow-moving clerk at the checkout counter seemed ___ to the fact that the line of impatient customers was growing longer and longer.

_______ 6. Some people who could benefit from counseling avoid seeing a therapist because they prefer to be ___ about private matters.

_______ 7. The cutting down of the rain forests has caused a dangerous rate of ___ among species that live in those forests.

_______ 8. Some days we're ___(e)d with junk email—it can take an hour to delete all the unwanted messages.

_______ 9. Alzheimer's disease is a disaster for the patient and a(n) ___ burden for the family.

_______ 10. If you want your essay to be ___, stick to your point.

NOTE: Now check your answers to these items by turning to page 129. Going over the answers carefully will help you prepare for the next two practices, for which answers are not given.

Sentence Check 2

Using the answer lines provided, complete each item below with **two** words from the box. Use each word once.

____
_______ 1–2. Child abuse is a(n) ___ crime, but children are often ___ about it. Their silence may prevent them from collaborating° with the police or the courts to bring the abusers to justice.

____
_______ 3–4. The company doesn't ___ the policy of laying off workers. It believes that the optimum° way to reduce the staff is by ___: employees who quit or retire simply aren't replaced.

____
_______ 5–6. Craig is ___(e)d with bills, but he continues to fritter° away his money. He's ___ to his financial problems.

_______________ 7–8. The teacher of the "Cooking for Health" class was ___ about avoiding egg yolks. "You don't need yolks for a(n) ___ batter!" he shouted. "The whites will hold it together."
____

_______________ 9–10. Although my brother was ___ enough to meet the army's standards for enlisting, his eyesight was too poor. He tried to ___ this problem by memorizing the eye chart.
____

Final Check: *Coco the Gorilla*

Here is a final opportunity for you to strengthen your knowledge of the ten words. First read the following selection carefully. Then fill in each blank with a word from the box at the top of the previous page. (Context clues will help you figure out which word goes in which blank.) Use each word once.

Illegal killings of gorillas are reducing their numbers far faster than would be expected from normal (1)_______________. Here is the story of one gorilla family.

Carrying spears and knives, hunters entered an African game preserve, where it was unlawful to kill or capture wildlife. When they spotted a young male gorilla, they closed in. Ten adult gorillas, members of a(n) (2)_______________ family group, attempted to shield the infant. The men quickly killed all the adult gorillas. As if (3)_______________ to the infant's screams, the men strapped his hands and feet to bamboo poles with wire, then carried him down the mountain on which he'd been born.

After several weeks, Dian Fossey, an American studying gorillas in the wild, learned that the young gorilla had been taken to park officials. She found him in a cage so small that he had no room to stand or turn. He was clearly frightened and nearly dead—thirsty, starving, and with infected wounds at his ankles and wrists. Fossey could hardly believe that the officials could (4)_______________ such reprehensible° cruelty.

When Fossey demanded an explanation from the park's chief official, he seemed (5)_______________ about the animal. Finally, however, he admitted that he had made an illegal deal with a German zoo. In return for a new car, he had arranged for the gorilla's capture. Fossey was (6)_______________ in insisting that the infant be released into her care. The official agreed on the condition that the infant be shipped to the zoo as soon as his health returned.

For several months, Fossey cared for the infant, now named Coco, who would cling to her for solace°. When he became more (7)_______________, he began to romp and explore. In an effort to (8)_______________ the agreement to send Coco to the zoo, Fossey (9)_______________(e)d government officials with letters, begging them to step in and arrange for him to be returned to the wild. In the end, though, the little gorilla was taken away from her—a(n) (10)_______________ hardship for both of them. Gorillas can live into their 50s, but Coco died in the zoo at the age of 12.

Scores Sentence Check 2 ________% Final Check ________%

Enter your scores above and in the **Vocabulary Performance Chart** on the inside back cover of the book.

bolster	**relegate**
depreciate	**replete**
indiscriminate	**sedentary**
inquisitive	**tenet**
nebulous	**terse**

Ten Words in Context

In the space provided, write the letter of the meaning closest to that of each **boldfaced** word. Use the context of the sentences to help you figure out each word's meaning.

1 bolster
(bōl′stər)
-verb

- The front porch was sagging, so we had to **bolster** it with cinder blocks until it could be repaired.
- When Yoko was in the hospital, visits from friends **bolstered** her spirits.

__ *Bolster* means A. to reach. B. to replace. C. to support.

2 depreciate
(dĭ-prē′shē-āt′)
-verb

- As soon as you drive a new car off the lot, it **depreciates**; it's immediately worth less than you paid for it.
- The property **depreciated** when the city built a sewage plant nearby.

__ *Depreciate* means A. to become better. B. to become less valuable. C. to become definite.

3 indiscriminate
(ĭn′dĭ-skrĭm′ĭ-nĭt)
-adjective

- Some people end up hopelessly in debt because of **indiscriminate** spending, so be selective about what and how much you buy.
- I confess to an **indiscriminate** love of chocolate. I don't distinguish between plain old Hershey bars and fancy imported chocolates—I adore them all.

__ *Indiscriminate* means A. healthy. B. unenthusiastic. C. not selective.

4 inquisitive
(ĭn-kwĭz′ə-tĭv)
-adjective

- **Inquisitive** students usually do better than those who are less curious and less eager to learn.
- Small children are naturally **inquisitive**. They wonder about the world around them, and they are constantly asking "Why?"

__ *Inquisitive* means A. hard-working. B. particular. C. questioning.

5 nebulous
(nĕb′yə-ləs)
-adjective

- Lenny's description of the car that fled the accident was **nebulous** and useless to police: "It was medium size and a dark color—maybe blue, black, gray, or even brown."
- "A good essay cannot be **nebulous**," the English instructor explained. "It must contain sharp, precise details."

__ *Nebulous* means A. indefinite. B. long. C. specific.

6 relegate
(rĕl′ə-gāt′)
-verb

- At family gatherings, we kids were always **relegated** to the kitchen table, while the adults ate in the dining room.
- When we have overnight guests, my parents give them my room and **relegate** me to a cot in the attic.

__ *Relegate* means A. to send. B. to punish. C. to reward.

7 replete
(rĭ-plēt′)
-adjective

- The show was **replete** with dazzling effects, including gorgeous scenery, glittering costumes, dramatic lighting, and thrilling music.
- The book of household hints got an excellent review. "It's **replete** with good advice," the critic wrote. "Every homeowner should purchase a copy."

__ *Replete* means A. replaced. B. filled. C. followed.

8 sedentary
(sĕd′n-tĕr′ē)
-adjective

- People in **sedentary** occupations, such as bus drivers and writers, need to make a special effort to exercise.
- My older sister's lifestyle is so **sedentary** that the longest walk she ever takes is from her living-room couch to the front seat of her car.

__ *Sedentary* means A. involving much walking. B. involving stress. C. involving much sitting.

9 tenet
(tĕn′ĭt)
-noun

- One of the basic **tenets** of democracy is freedom of speech.
- This world might be a paradise if everyone lived by such **tenets** as "Never cause suffering."

__ *Tenet* means A. a principle. B. a ritual. C. a prediction.

10 terse
(tûrs)
-adjective

- I was hurt by Roberto's **terse** response to my invitation. All he said was "No thanks."
- A British humor magazine once gave this **terse** advice to people about to marry: "Don't."

__ *Terse* means A. dishonest. B. unclear. C. short.

Matching Words with Definitions

Following are definitions of the ten words. Clearly write or print each word next to its definition. The sentences above and on the previous page will help you decide on the meaning of each word.

1. ____________ To fall or decrease in value or price; to lower the value of
2. ____________ Not chosen carefully; not based on careful selection
3. ____________ Marked by much sitting; requiring or taking little exercise
4. ____________ A belief or principle held to be true by an individual or group
5. ____________ Brief and clear; effectively concise
6. ____________ To hold up, strengthen, or reinforce; support with a rigid object
7. ____________ Curious; eager to learn
8. ____________ Plentifully supplied; well-filled
9. ____________ Vague; unclear
10. ____________ To assign to a less important or less satisfying position, place, or condition

CAUTION: Do not go any further until you are sure the above answers are correct. Then you can use the definitions to help you in the following practices. Your goal is eventually to know the words well enough so that you don't need to check the definitions at all.

Sentence Check 1

Using the answer line provided, complete each item below with the correct word from the box. Use each word once.

A. **bolster**	B. **depreciate**	C. **indiscriminate**	D. **inquisitive**	E. **nebulous**
F. **relegate**	G. **replete**	H. **sedentary**	I. **tenet**	J. **terse**

______ 1. A large sign in the boys' treehouse stated their club's main ___: "No Girls or Snakes Allowed!!!"

______ 2. Houses and antiques often increase in value as they get older, but most other things, like cars, computers, and appliances, tend to ___.

______ 3. When a sofa leg broke, we ___(e)d that end of the sofa with a pile of books.

______ 4. Phan's TV viewing is ___. He just watches whatever happens to be on.

______ 5. John considers Arlene rude because her comments are usually ___, but I prefer her brief, clear answers to his long-winded ones.

______ 6. The book *Answers to 1,001 Interesting Questions* sounds like the perfect gift for a(n) ___ person.

______ 7. When we were children, my active sister was always playing tag or jumping rope. I was more ___, preferring to spend hour after hour just sitting and reading.

______ 8. Before this semester, my thoughts about a career were ___, but now I have a much clearer idea of what work I want to do.

______ 9. The catcher worried that unless he started playing better, he'd be ___(e)d to the minor leagues.

______ 10. The refrigerator was ___ with all kinds of marvelous foods for the party.

NOTE: Now check your answers to these items by turning to page 129. Going over the answers carefully will help you prepare for the next two practices, for which answers are not given.

Sentence Check 2

Using the answer lines provided, complete each item below with **two** words from the box. Use each word once.

______
______ 1–2. The guides at the Leaning Tower of Pisa are inundated° with questions from ___ travelers: "Why is it leaning?" "How far is it leaning?" "Is it being ___(e)d to keep it from falling any further?"

______
______ 3–4. Dad was a construction worker, but as soon as he reached 60—though he was as robust° as ever—his company ___(e)d him to a(n) ___ desk job.

______
______ 5–6. When my parents bought their new house, they asked the real estate agent whether it was likely to increase in value or ___. The agent gave this ___ answer: "It's always hard to tell about these things."

_______________ 7–8. Stan is not exactly a(n) ___ speaker, which is why he's earned the nickname "Motor Mouth." What's more, his conversation is totally ___; he uses no discretion° but just says anything that comes to mind.
____

_______________ 9–10. Folk wisdom is ___ with contradictory sayings and ___s. It's fun to juxtapose° pairs such as "He who hesitates is lost" and "Look before you leap."
____

Final Check: *Our Annual Garage Sale*

Here is a final opportunity for you to strengthen your knowledge of the ten words. First read the following selection carefully. Then fill in each blank with a word from the box at the top of the previous page. (Context clues will help you figure out which word goes in which blank.) Use each word once.

It's almost September—time for our annual garage sale. Since we hate to relinquish° anything we've spent money on, we have a large supply of unwanted items. They keep piling up in the basement, which is now so full that we've had to (1)_______________ some of the collection to the garage. Though the sale is a lot of work, the sight of all those piles and boxes (2)_______________s our determination to go through with it.

© Agata Dorobek/shutterstock.com

This stockpiling of stuff has left us with a huge number of possessions for sale, from tools and spools to baskets and gaskets. This year, for example, we have an old bike that some zealot° for exercise might buy and a soft chair and footstool for a more (3)_______________ customer. Our ad states our main (4)_______________: "Something for everyone!" Maybe that's a bit (5)_______________, but we don't want to be specific. We just want to communicate the general idea that our sale will be (6)_______________ with treasures.

Last year, one customer took a quick look and departed with the (7)_______________ comment "Nothing but junk." However, most people seem to take a completely (8)_______________ approach to shopping. They're predisposed° to spend their money on anything that's a bargain, even if it isn't in optimum° condition—such as rusty baking pans and broken lamps. Then there are the (9)_______________ shoppers who want us to tell them every detail about every item: How old is it? What did we pay for it? Will it increase in value, or will it (10)_______________?

Friends have foolishly asked us where in the world we get all this junk to sell year after year—an inane° question, because the answer is simple. We shop at garage sales.

Scores Sentence Check 2 _______% Final Check _______%

Enter your scores above and in the **Vocabulary Performance Chart** on the inside back cover of the book.

clandestine	**indigenous**
contingency	**liability**
egocentric	**prolific**
exonerate	**reinstate**
incongruous	**superfluous**

Ten Words in Context

In the space provided, write the letter of the meaning closest to that of each **boldfaced** word. Use the context of the sentences to help you figure out each word's meaning.

1 clandestine
(klăn-dĕs'tĭn)
-adjective

- In a **clandestine** meeting in an alley, Steve sold his employer's valuable anti-aging formula to a competitor.
- The famous "Underground Railroad" was not an actual railroad; it was a **clandestine** network that took escaped slaves to safety in the years before the Civil War.

__ *Clandestine* means A. popular. B. unnecessary. C. secret.

2 contingency
(kən-tĭn'jən-sē)
-noun

- Faye thought her company might transfer her to another city. With that **contingency** in mind, she decided to rent a house rather than buy one.
- We believe in providing for every **contingency**. We have a list of emergency phone numbers, a first-aid kit, and a box of candles in case of a power failure.

__ *Contingency* means A. a possibility. B. an advantage. C. a desire.

3 egocentric
(ē'gō-sĕn'trĭk)
-adjective

- Denise is completely **egocentric**. Whatever event takes place, she thinks only of how it will affect her personally.
- "We've talked enough about me," said the **egocentric** author to a friend. "Now let's talk about you. What do you think of my new book?"

__ *Egocentric* means A. selfish. B. considerate. C. self-educated.

4 exonerate
(ĕg-zŏn'ər-āt')
-verb

- Saul was suspected of shoplifting, but he was **exonerated** when a security camera showed another man taking handfuls of batteries from a rack and stuffing them into his backpack.
- Politicians accused of illegal activities always seem to say the same thing: that they'll be **exonerated** when all the facts are known.

__ *Exonerate* means A. to be harmed. B. to be found guilty. C. to be found not guilty.

5 incongruous
(ĭn-kŏng'grŏŏ-əs)
-adjective

- The cuckoo lays eggs in other birds' nests. This practice can result in the **incongruous** sight of one large cuckoo chick among several tiny baby robins.
- It wasn't really **incongruous** for a former general to join the peace movement. He had seen the horrors of war.

__ *Incongruous* means A. contradictory. B. unnecessary. C. not noticeable.

6 indigenous
(ĭn-dĭj'ə-nəs)
-adjective

- Kangaroos are **indigenous** only to Australia. They have never been found living anywhere else in the world.
- Corn was not **indigenous** to Europe, so Europeans had never seen or heard of it until their explorers first reached the New World and found it growing there.

__ *Indigenous* means A. important. B. native. C. welcomed.

7 liability
(lī′ə-bĭl′ə-tē)
-noun

- My shyness with strangers would be a **liability** in any job that involved meeting the public, such as sales.
- When Juanita returned to school at age 40, she was afraid her age would be a **liability**. Instead, she found that it gave her an advantage over younger students.

__ *Liability* means A. an asset. B. a handicap. C. a necessity.

8 prolific
(prō-lĭf′ĭk)
-adjective

- Rabbits deserve their reputation for being **prolific**. A female rabbit can produce three families each summer.
- Haydn was a **prolific** composer. He wrote, among many other musical works, 104 symphonies.

__ *Prolific* means A. creating abundantly. B. working secretly. C. important.

9 reinstate
(rē′ĭn-stāt′)
-verb

- Michiko left work for a year to stay home with her new baby. When she returned, she was relieved and happy to be **reinstated** in her former job.
- The college had canceled the course in folklore, but the demand was so great that the class had to be **reinstated**.

__ *Reinstate* means A. to recognize. B. to appreciate. C. to put back.

10 superfluous
(sŏŏ-pûr′flōō-əs)
-adjective

- The tiny horns on a giraffe's head are **superfluous**. Scientists have concluded that the horns serve absolutely no purpose at all.
- Lately, business at the store has been so slow that the three clerks have almost nothing to do. Two of them seem **superfluous**.

__ *Superfluous* means A. unnecessary. B. ordinary. C. required.

Matching Words with Definitions

Following are definitions of the ten words. Clearly write or print each word next to its definition. The sentences above and on the previous page will help you decide on the meaning of each word.

1. ____________ Something that acts as a disadvantage; a drawback
2. ____________ Done in secret; kept hidden
3. ____________ Out of place; having parts that are not in harmony or that are inconsistent
4. ____________ A possible future event that must be prepared for or guarded against; possibility
5. ____________ Living, growing, or produced naturally in a particular place; native
6. ____________ Beyond what is needed, wanted, or useful; extra
7. ____________ Producing many works, results, or offspring; fertile
8. ____________ To clear of an accusation or charge; prove innocent
9. ____________ Self-centered; seeing everything in terms of oneself
10. ____________ To restore to a previous position or condition; bring back into being or use

CAUTION: Do not go any further until you are sure the above answers are correct. Then you can use the definitions to help you in the following practices. Your goal is eventually to know the words well enough so that you don't need to check the definitions at all.

Sentence Check 1

Using the answer line provided, complete each item below with the correct word from the box. Use each word once.

A. **clandestine**	B. **contingency**	C. **egocentric**	D. **exonerate**	E. **incongruous**
F. **indigenous**	G. **liability**	H. **prolific**	I. **reinstate**	J. **superfluous**

__________ 1. Although our city has never been struck by an earthquake, it has emergency plans for just such a ___.

__________ 2. Gardens in the desert usually feature ___ plants, such as cactus. Native plants thrive in dry heat and need little watering.

__________ 3. Bad handwriting is not a serious ___ in this age of smartphones and computers.

__________ 4. Sharon and Eli have ___(e)d a Jewish family tradition they hadn't observed for years: lighting candles on the Sabbath.

__________ 5. Agnes is only five feet tall, but her boyfriend is six-foot-four. They make a(n) ___-looking couple.

__________ 6. Nancy is so ___ that when I told her my car had been stolen, her only reaction was, "Does this mean you can't drive me to work tomorrow?"

__________ 7. "Your writing is too wordy," the teacher had written on my paper. "Eliminate all those ___ words and phrases."

__________ 8. Because a submarine is able to hide under water, it can be very useful in ___ operations.

__________ 9. Flies are amazingly ___. Within a five-month breeding period, one female can produce thousands of offspring.

__________ 10. Two students were blamed for starting the fire in the physics lab, but they were ___(e)d when it was found that the cause was faulty electrical equipment.

NOTE: Now check your answers to these items by turning to page 129. Going over the answers carefully will help you prepare for the next two practices, for which answers are not given.

Sentence Check 2

Using the answer lines provided, complete each item below with **two** words from the box. Use each word once.

____
__________ 1–2. The ___ author has just had her fiftieth novel published. Although she has written numerous books, her writing style remains tight, with no ___ words.

____
__________ 3–4. When one million dollars mysteriously vanished, the company decided to fire its accountant. But he was ___(e)d and ___(e)d in his position when the cause was discovered to be a computer malfunction.

____
__________ 5–6. People who spend Christmas in Florida often find the decorations ___. Santa Clauses, sleighs, reindeer, and fir trees somehow seem ___ to the North and look odd juxtaposed° with palm trees and tropical flowers.

____________________ 7–8. The ship's captain seemed to be losing his mental balance. Fearing that he might become completely insane, the crew held a(n) ____ meeting to discuss what to do in that ____.
____

____________________ 9–10. The foreman is so ____ that he has become a ____ to the company. Concerned only with his own needs, he's oblivious° to the needs of the workers.
____

Final Check: *My Large Family*

Here is a final opportunity for you to strengthen your knowledge of the ten words. First read the following selection carefully. Then fill in each blank with a word from the box at the top of the previous page. (Context clues will help you figure out which word goes in which blank.) Use each word once.

For many years I didn't realize that my family was larger than normal. That's because enormous families somehow seemed (1)____________________ to our neighborhood. I don't know what made people on our block so (2)____________________, but the Harrisons, who lived on one side of us, had nine kids; and the Montoyas, on the other side, had twelve. When Mom said she was going to have her eleventh child, the ten of us wondered if another baby wasn't (3)____________________: one more than necessary. Still, I think we enjoyed one another as much as any family I know. Naturally, we had our battles, but though they were sometimes intense, they never lasted long, and it didn't take much to (4)____________________ yourself in a brother's or a sister's good graces. If nothing else worked, you could always (5)____________________ yourself by blaming whatever had happened on another sibling who wasn't home at the moment. Also, we learned to cooperate. When you have to get along with so many different people, you learn not to be (6)____________________. A self-centered person wouldn't have lasted ten minutes in my home.

Of course, there were times when the size of our family was a (7)____________________. With all those people around, any kind of (8)____________________ activity was just about impossible—there was simply no place to hide and no way to keep a secret. Our numbers could be a detriment°, as well. Once, a new neighbor, not realizing how many of us there were, offered to take us all for ice cream. With amusement, he watched the (9)____________________ sight of nine children and one toddler trying to squeeze into an ordinary passenger car. Although he obviously hadn't been prepared for such a (10)____________________, it didn't squelch° his plans. He just grinned and said, "Okay, we'll go in shifts."

Scores Sentence Check 2 ________% Final Check ________%

Enter your scores above and in the **Vocabulary Performance Chart** on the inside back cover of the book.

austere	**metamorphosis**
esoteric	**notorious**
facsimile	**perfunctory**
grotesque	**provocative**
mesmerize	**travesty**

Ten Words in Context

In the space provided, write the letter of the meaning closest to that of each **boldfaced** word. Use the context of the sentences to help you figure out each word's meaning.

1 austere
(ô-stîr′)
-adjective

- Ms. Stone's appearance was **austere**. She wore plain, dark-colored clothing with no jewelry, and she never used makeup.
- The walls in Mario's den are white and nearly bare, and his white furniture has simple lines. This **austere** decor gives the room a pleasantly calm mood.

__ *Austere* means   A. very ugly.   B. very plain.   C. very youthful.

2 esoteric
(ĕs′ə-tĕr′ĭk)
-adjective

- The lecture "Is There Life On Other Planets?" sounded interesting, but it was so **esoteric** that only a few scientists in the audience understood it.
- The poetry of Ezra Pound, filled with references to ancient Greek culture, is too **esoteric** for most readers.

__ *Esoteric* means   A. difficult to understand.   B. shallow.   C. unfavorable.

3 facsimile
(făk-sĭm′ə-lē)
-noun

- When a **facsimile** of an old Sears-Roebuck shopping catalog was published, it became a bestseller. People enjoyed seeing what was for sale a century ago.
- The little girl was amazed to see a famous painting on the classroom wall. "That's the *Mona Lisa*!" she said. Of course, it was a **facsimile**, not the original.

__ *Facsimile* means   A. an original.   B. a distorted version.   C. an accurate copy.

4 grotesque
(grō-tĕsk′)
-adjective

- Some breeds of cats are hairless. Some people find their bare pink skin adorable, but I think they look **grotesque**.
- The clown made **grotesque** faces, squinting his eyes, pulling down the corners of his mouth, and sticking out his tongue.

__ *Grotesque* means   A. strange-looking.   B. hard to understand.   C. charming.

5 mesmerize
(mĕz′mə-rīz′)
-verb

- The intense eyes of the woman in the photograph **mesmerized** me. I couldn't take my eyes off the picture.
- The toddler was **mesmerized** by the fish tank and stood in front of it, gazing at the fish for nearly an hour.

__ *Mesmerize* means   A. to amuse.   B. to fascinate.   C. to distort.

6 metamorphosis
(mĕt′ə-môr′fə-sĭs)
-noun

- A caterpillar's transformation into a butterfly is a well-known example of **metamorphosis**.
- In Franz Kafka's famous story "The **Metamorphosis**," a man wakes up on his thirtieth birthday to discover that he has turned into an enormous insect.

__ *Metamorphosis* means   A. a change in form.   B. a disaster.   C. a scientific theory.

7 notorious
(nō-tôr′ē-əs)
-adjective

- Batman and Robin matched wits with the Joker and the Penguin, who were **notorious** for their evil deeds.
- The local diner is **notorious** for bitter coffee, soggy vegetables, limp salads, and mystery meat.

___ *Notorious* means A. regarded negatively. B. regarded with curiosity. C. ignored.

8 perfunctory
(pər-fŭnk′tə-rē)
-adjective

- The doctor's examination was **perfunctory**. He seemed to be just going through the motions without taking any interest in the patient.
- Most of the candidates were passionate on the subject of nuclear weapons, but one spoke in a very **perfunctory** way, apparently bored with the topic.

___ *Perfunctory* means A. uninterested. B. enthusiastic. C. exaggerated.

9 provocative
(prō-vŏk′ə-tĭv)
-adjective

- "A good essay is **provocative**," said our English instructor. "It gets the reader interested and attentive, starting with the very first paragraph."
- To arouse the viewers' curiosity, the television ad began with a **provocative** image: a spaceship landing on a baseball field, at home plate.

___ *Provocative* means A. predictable. B. difficult to understand. C. attention-getting.

10 travesty
(trăv′ĭs-tē)
-noun

- The election was a **travesty**. Voters were threatened to support the current leader, so it was anything but a genuine, fair process.
- The musical-comedy version of *Hamlet* was a **travesty**. The critics and audience agreed that it made a mockery of Shakespeare's profound tragedy.

___ *Travesty* means A. a disrespectful imitation. B. an exact copy. C. a simple version.

Matching Words with Definitions

Following are definitions of the ten words. Clearly write or print each word next to its definition. The sentences above and on the previous page will help you decide on the meaning of each word.

1. ____________ To hypnotize or fascinate; hold spellbound
2. ____________ A great or complete change; transformation
3. ____________ A crude, exaggerated, or ridiculous representation; mockery
4. ____________ Done only as a routine, with little care or interest; performed with no interest or enthusiasm
5. ____________ Known widely but unfavorably; having a bad reputation
6. ____________ Tending to arouse interest or curiosity
7. ____________ An exact copy or reproduction
8. ____________ Intended for or understood by only a certain group; beyond the understanding of most people
9. ____________ Without decoration or luxury; severely simple
10. ____________ Distorted or strikingly inconsistent in shape, appearance, or manner

CAUTION: Do not go any further until you are sure the above answers are correct. Then you can use the definitions to help you in the following practices. Your goal is eventually to know the words well enough so that you don't need to check the definitions at all.

Sentence Check 1

Using the answer line provided, complete each item below with the correct word from the box. Use each word once.

A. austere	B. esoteric	C. facsimile	D. grotesque	E. mesmerize
F. metamorphosis	G. notorious	H. perfunctory	I. provocative	J. travesty

______ 1. Lining the music school's hallway are framed ___s of handwritten pages of music by great composers.

______ 2. In some modern paintings, human figures are distorted into such ___ shapes that it's hard to recognize facial features and body parts.

______ 3. To capture readers' attention, an author sometimes begins an article with a(n) ___ question, such as, "Which do you think is more dangerous, climbing stairs or parachuting out of an airplane?"

______ 4. King Henry VIII of England was ___ not only for getting married six times, but also for having two of his wives executed.

______ 5. The trial was a ___ of justice because several of the jurors had been bribed.

______ 6. The magician David Copperfield performed a trick called "___." One person was chained and locked in a box. When the box was opened, that person was gone, and someone else was chained there instead.

______ 7. My sister's dormitory room is rather ___, with cement-block walls and bare floors, but she's made it less stark by hanging colorful posters and adding bright bedspreads and cushions.

______ 8. Usually the therapist showed great interest in her patients, but today she was too worried about her own family to give more than ___ responses.

______ 9. As I stood looking at the grandfather clock, I became ___(e)d by the shiny pendulum that swung back and forth, back and forth, back and forth.

______ 10. Legal documents are usually worded in such ___ language that most people need a lawyer to translate the "legalese" into plain English.

NOTE: Now check your answers to these items by turning to page 130. Going over the answers carefully will help you prepare for the next two practices, for which answers are not given.

Sentence Check 2

Using the answer lines provided, complete each item below with **two** words from the box. Use each word once.

______
______ 1–2. The cat burglar in the film, ___ for stealing expensive jewelry, committed all his robberies wearing a(n) ___ outfit: a black T-shirt, plain black pants, black shoes, and black gloves.

______
______ 3–4. The monkey house at the zoo was ___. The poor monkeys were crowded into a concrete room with palm trees painted on the wall—a ___ of a "jungle" environment.

____________________ 5–6. At the jewelers' convention, ___s of several famous gems were on display. I enjoyed seeing them, but I didn't understand the accompanying ___ explanation of the technical methods used to produce the copies.
____

____________________ 7–8. Former principals had made only ___ efforts to rid the high school of drugs, but the new principal, supported by the parents' association, attacked the problem head-on. As a result, the school has undergone a ___ from "hooked" to "clean."
____

____________________ 9–10. The novel has a(n) ___ opening scene, in which a young woman and her parrot sneak out of a house on a ladder. The novel goes on to ___ the reader with one spellbinding episode after another.
____

Final Check: *A Costume Party*

Here is a final opportunity for you to strengthen your knowledge of the ten words. First read the following selection carefully. Then fill in each blank with a word from the box at the top of the previous page. (Context clues will help you figure out which word goes in which blank.) Use each word once.

On the afternoon of a friend's New Year's Eve costume party, I made only a(n) (1)____________________ effort to put a costume together. Unenthusiastic about spending much time on this, I wanted to create something as simple and rudimentary° as possible, even if the effect would be rather (2)____________________. I decided on a ghost costume—just a plain sheet with eyeholes cut out. Since all my sheets are green, I had to be the ghost of a frog.

© David Pereiras/shutterstock.com

The party began for me with a (3)____________________ encounter: the door was opened by Jennifer Lawrence, smiling flirtatiously and clutching her Best Actress Oscar—or at least an excellent (4)____________________ of it. Then, when I went inside, the first men I saw were two (5)____________________ pirates, Blackbeard and Captain Hook. I listened in on their conversation, expecting to be (6)____________________(e)d by fascinating tales of cut-throat adventures; instead, I heard only the (7)____________________ language of two math majors.

Giving up any hope of understanding their remarks, I looked around for my own friends. But their (8)____________________ from ordinary people to famous or odd people was so complete that I couldn't recognize anyone. Most of the costumes were in good taste. One, though, struck me as a (9)____________________: a person dressed as Abraham Lincoln—a President I venerate° for his character and leadership—was wearing a bull's-eye target, in crude mockery of President Lincoln's assassination. Another person looked frighteningly (10)____________________, with a mouth twisted to one side and three eyes, all of different sizes.

In the course of the evening, I also met Cleopatra, Shakespeare, and Snoopy, among others. I may never again spend time at a gathering replete° with so many celebrities.

Scores Sentence Check 2 _________% Final Check _________%

Enter your scores above and in the **Vocabulary Performance Chart** on the inside back cover of the book.

CHAPTER 10

connoisseur	lucid
conspiracy	plight
contrite	superficially
distraught	symmetrical
germane	verbose

Ten Words in Context

In the space provided, write the letter of the meaning closest to that of each **boldfaced** word. Use the context of the sentences to help you figure out each word's meaning.

1 connoisseur
(kŏn′ə-sûr′)
-noun

- My sister is a **connoisseur** of Southern novels. She's read dozens of them, and she knows all about the authors and their different styles.
- Curtis has broad knowledge of French wines—where they are made, when they are at their best, and exactly how each one tastes. He's a true **connoisseur**.

__ *Connoisseur* means A. a doubter. B. an authority. C. a leader.

2 conspiracy
(kən-spĭr′ə-sē)
-noun

- The **conspiracy** to overthrow the government was started by two of the premier's own advisors.
- Although only Lee Harvey Oswald was arrested for the assassination of President Kennedy, many believe there was a **conspiracy** to kill the president.

__ *Conspiracy* means A. a plot. B. an idea. C. an announcement.

3 contrite
(kən-trīt′)
-adjective

- Dolores was especially **contrite** about tearing her sister's dress because she'd borrowed it without permission.
- Judges are often more lenient with offenders who truly regret their crimes. A criminal who seems genuinely **contrite** may get a shorter sentence.

__ *Contrite* means A. angry. B. confused. C. sorry.

4 distraught
(dĭ-strôt′)
-adjective

- The parents of the little girl who wandered off in the crowded mall were **distraught** until she was found.
- Darrell was so **distraught** when his grandfather died that he spent an entire week looking through old pictures and crying.

__ *Distraught* means A. upset. B. busy. C. forgetful.

5 germane
(jər-mān′)
-adjective

- Stacy went to the law library to look up information that might be **germane** to her client's case.
- It bothered Christine when her new boss asked if she had a boyfriend. That information certainly wasn't **germane** to her work.

__ *Germane* means A. damaging. B. related. C. foreign.

6 lucid
(lo͞o′sĭd)
-adjective

- I usually find furniture assembly instructions horribly unclear, but these are **lucid**.
- The scientist's explanation of climate change was so **lucid** that the entire audience was able to grasp it.

__ *Lucid* means A. easy to understand. B. repetitious. C. fair to both sides.

7 plight
(plīt)
-noun

- The **plight** of the homeless can be somewhat relieved by decent shelters.
- There were reports of a cave-in at the mine, but it was too soon to know much about the **plight** of the trapped miners.

__ *Plight* means A. a delayed situation. B. an unlikely situation. C. an unfortunate situation.

8 superficially
(so͞o′pər-fĭsh′əl-lē)
-adverb

- Nina spent a full week studying for the exam. Joyce, however, reviewed **superficially**, flipping through the pages of her textbook an hour before the test.
- This morning, the mechanic was short of time and inspected my car only **superficially**. He said he'd check it thoroughly later and then give me an estimate.

__ *Superficially* means A. thoroughly. B. slightly. C. daily.

9 symmetrical
(sĭ-mĕt′rĭ-kəl)
-adjective

- The children's sandcastle was **symmetrical**, with a wall on each side and a tower and flag at each end.
- No one's face is perfectly **symmetrical**. For example, one eye is usually slightly higher than the other, and the left and right sides of the mouth differ.

__ *Symmetrical* means A. unique. B. beautiful. C. balanced.

10 verbose
(vər-bōs′)
-adjective

- The **verbose** senator said, "At this point in time, we have an urgent and important need for more monetary funds to declare unconditional war on drugs and combat this evil and harmful situation." The reporter wrote, "The senator said we urgently need more money to fight drugs."
- Gabe is the most **verbose** person I know. He always uses ten words when one would do.

__ *Verbose* means A. loud. B. wordy. C. self-important.

Matching Words with Definitions

Following are definitions of the ten words. Clearly write or print each word next to its definition. The sentences above and on the previous page will help you decide on the meaning of each word.

1. ____________ Very troubled; distressed
2. ____________ Using or containing too many words
3. ____________ In an on-the-surface manner; not thoroughly
4. ____________ Having to do with the issue at hand; relevant
5. ____________ Clearly expressed; easily understood
6. ____________ Truly sorry for having done wrong; repentant
7. ____________ Well proportioned; balanced; the same on both sides
8. ____________ An expert in fine art or in matters of taste
9. ____________ A situation marked by difficulty, hardship, or misfortune
10. ____________ A secret plot by two or more people, especially for a harmful or illegal purpose

CAUTION: Do not go any further until you are sure the above answers are correct. Then you can use the definitions to help you in the following practices. Your goal is eventually to know the words well enough so that you don't need to check the definitions at all.

Sentence Check 1

Using the answer line provided, complete each item below with the correct word from the box. Use each word once.

A. **connoisseur**	B. **conspiracy**	C. **contrite**	D. **distraught**	E. **germane**
F. **lucid**	G. **plight**	H. **superficially**	I. **symmetrical**	J. **verbose**

________________ 1. In writing, it is actually easier to be ___ than to make the effort to cut out the unnecessary words.

________________ 2. A ___ of Asian art told me that my Chinese vase is very old, quite rare, and valuable.

________________ 3. The garden is ___, with the same flowers and shrubs, arranged in the same pattern, on each side of a central path.

________________ 4. Everyone is greatly concerned about the ___ of the hostages. We're not even certain they're still alive.

________________ 5. Nadia was truly sorry for having started the argument with Reese. To show how ___ she felt, she texted him a lengthy apology.

________________ 6. Whenever Miki tries to buy a new dress, her husband is only ___ interested. If she shows him one and asks his opinion, all he says is, "It's fine. Let's buy it and get out of here."

________________ 7. Ved's teacher was so pleased with his clear explanation of a difficult theory that she wrote on his paper, "Wonderfully ___!"

________________ 8. My parents had expected my sister home by ten o'clock. By the time she finally walked in at two in the morning, they were very ___.

________________ 9. The teacher and the other students became irritated when Susan kept asking questions that weren't ___ to the class discussion.

________________ 10. During the Revolutionary War, Benedict Arnold, an American officer, was involved in a ___ to help the British win.

NOTE: Now check your answers to these items by turning to page 130. Going over the answers carefully will help you prepare for the next two practices, for which answers are not given.

Sentence Check 2

Using the answer lines provided, complete each item below with **two** words from the box. Use each word once.

____
________________ 1–2. The drunk driver is ___ about causing the accident, but his regret won't give Marsha solace° or ease her ___. She is permanently disabled.

____
________________ 3–4. Ms. Lewis is a ___ of Native American crafts. She can identify the tribe of the artist after examining a necklace or piece of pottery only ___.

____
________________ 5–6. In the horror movie, the heroine becomes more and more ___ as she realizes that her husband and friends are involved in a ___ against her.

______________ 7–8. Using excess words can make something more difficult to understand. Thus if the essay had not been so ___, it would have been more ___.
____

______________ 9–10. The professor said, "It seems ___ to our discussion of the Age of Reason to mention that ___ architecture was typical. Balance was valued—both in art and in the individual."
____

Final Check: *The Missing Painting*

Here is a final opportunity for you to strengthen your knowledge of the ten words. First read the following selection carefully. Then fill in each blank with a word from the box at the top of the previous page. (Context clues will help you figure out which word goes in which blank.) Use each word once.

© cunaplus/shutterstock.com

It wasn't until noon that Daniel Cobb noticed that the painting was missing. He immediately became (1)______________. As a (2)______________ of art, he was well aware of the enormous value of the painting—and this was a grievous° loss. He was so upset that when he phoned the police, he could not think or talk clearly enough to give a (3)______________ description of his unfortunate (4)______________. Instead, he found himself rambling so much that he was afraid the police would think he was just a (5)______________ old fool.

Nevertheless, the police soon arrived at Cobb's home, which was magnificent—a fine old mansion with a (6)______________ entrance, featuring a row of columns on each side of the front door. Leading the police to the room from which the painting had been taken, Cobb began to explain. "Last night," he said, "my wife and I gave a dinner party for art experts. We showed them our entire collection. I remember that they gave the missing painting special attention. At least, a few of them seemed to look at it more than just (7)______________. I can only assume that we are the victims of a (8)______________. Our guests must have plotted a clandestine° action: to sneak into the house during the night and take the painting."

As Cobb finished speaking, his wife entered the room, having just returned from town. She was clearly alarmed by the presence of the police. After Cobb quickly repeated his story, however, she started to laugh. "Today's Monday," she finally said.

"I hardly see how that's (9)______________ to our problem!" her husband responded.

"Remember, we told the Leeworth Art Association it could exhibit the painting today, for its annual show. That's where I've been. I took the painting there early this morning."

Cobb looked embarrassed but relieved that his guests had been exonerated° by his wife's story. "Accept my sincere apology for having bothered you. I am most (10)______________," he said to the police officers. "Please stay and have some lunch."

Scores Sentence Check 2 ________% Final Check ________%

Enter your scores above and in the **Vocabulary Performance Chart** on the inside back cover of the book.

UNIT TWO: Review

The box at the right lists twenty-five words from Unit Two. Using the clues at the bottom of the page, fill in these words to complete the puzzle that follows.

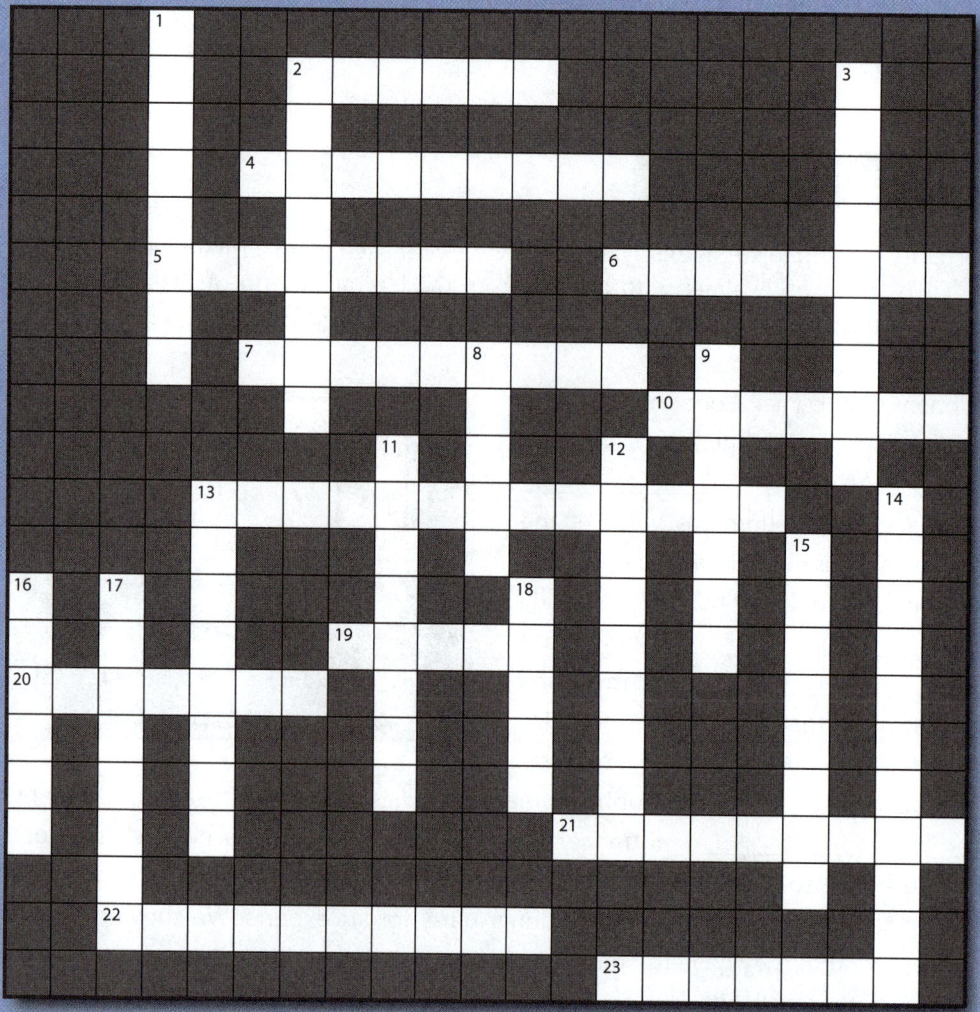

attrition
austere
bolster
clandestine
contrite
egocentric
esoteric
facsimile
inundate
liability
lucid
notorious
plight
prolific
reinstate
relegate
replete
reticent
robust
sanction
superficially
tenet
terse
travesty
verbose

ACROSS

2. A situation marked by difficulty or misfortune
4. Known widely but unfavorably
5. Quiet; reluctant to speak out
6. Truly sorry for having done wrong; repentant
7. Something that acts as a disadvantage; a drawback
10. Using or containing too many words
13. Not thoroughly
19. Brief; clear; concise
20. To support or reinforce
21. To restore to a previous position or condition
22. Self-centered; seeing everything in terms of oneself
23. Without decoration or luxury; severely simple

DOWN

1. Intended for or understood only by a certain group
2. Producing many works, results, or offspring
3. A gradual natural decrease in number
8. Clearly expressed; easily understood
9. Plentifully supplied
11. A crude, exaggerated, or ridiculous representation; a mockery
12. An exact copy
13. To authorize or approve
14. Done in secret; kept hidden
15. To cover, as by flooding; overwhelm with a large number or amount
16. Healthy and strong; vigorous
17. To assign to a less important or less satisfying position
18. A belief or principle held to be true by an individual or group

UNIT TWO: Test 1

PART A

Choose the word that best completes each item and write it in the space provided.

______________ 1. A modern American wedding is ___ with customs originally intended to ensure the couple's fertility, including having a wedding cake, throwing rice, and tying shoes to the back of the car.

A. verbose B. inquisitive C. replete D. grievous

______________ 2. The Englishman John Merrick had an illness that gave him a ___ appearance, which is why he was called "The Elephant Man." Despite people's reactions to his misshapen head and body, Merrick remained affectionate and gentle.

A. germane B. superfluous C. contrite D. grotesque

______________ 3. Toshio seems so ___ today that it's hard to believe he was close to death only two months ago.

A. robust B. terse C. austere D. grievous

______________ 4. Having lived in Italy and studied cooking there, the newspaper's food critic is a ___ of Italian cuisine.

A. facsimile B. sanction C. plight D. connoisseur

______________ 5. March is ___ for its extreme weather, which can include blizzards, flooding rains, tornadoes, and calm spring days.

A. reticent B. symmetrical C. notorious D. incongruous

______________ 6. Some people feel that a circus act in which costumed elephants dance or stand on their heads is a ___ of these intelligent animals' true nature.

A. liability B. facsimile C. conspiracy D. travesty

______________ 7. Because of the ___ nature of drug dealing, it is very difficult to stop. Most of the transactions take place on dark street corners or behind closed doors.

A. terse B. clandestine C. sedentary D. inquisitive

______________ 8. The managers at Brian's company refused to ___ the early-retirement plan proposed by the union because they felt the plan would cost too much.

A. relegate B. sanction C. inundate D. circumvent

______________ 9. My friends and I are a ___ group. We stick together through good times and bad.

A. prolific B. germane C. cohesive D. terse

______________ 10. In almost any job, being unable to read is a definite ___.

A. contingency B. facsimile C. tenet D. liability

(Continues on next page)

PART B

On the answer line, write the letter of the choice that best completes each item.

_____ 11. The police officer was **superficially** wounded, so the doctor
- A. rushed him to the hospital for immediate surgery.
- B. suggested that he call his family and clergyperson.
- C. put on a bandage and told him he could return to work.
- D. asked to consult with a specialist.

_____ 12. Because the new morning talk show was not attracting a large audience, it was **relegated** to
- A. 9 p.m., when it could compete with the most popular shows.
- B. a new host with a more sparkling personality.
- C. a reality series featuring a new kind of danger every week.
- D. 1:30 a.m., when few people would be watching.

_____ 13. Which of the following phrases contains a **superfluous** word?
- A. “A big huge whale.”
- B. “A small red chicken.”
- C. “A frisky young dog.”
- D. “A beautiful black cat.”

_____ 14. Lilian is extremely **reticent** about her private life. As a result, I
- A. know almost nothing about it.
- B. know every detail of her private life.
- C. really get tired of her bragging.
- D. worry that she trusts the wrong people.

_____ 15. The **austere** office
- A. had bare walls, a small desk, and one chair.
- B. was filled with desks and file cabinets.
- C. contained fake flowers and cheap posters.
- D. had fine art, live plants, and plush carpets.

_____ 16. Which of the following is an example of **attrition**?
- A. The number of students enrolled in the algebra class remained the same all semester.
- B. The population in our town has increased so much we’ve had to build a second school.
- C. In January we had a single pair of mice; by December we had 55 adults and babies.
- D. Our 20-year class reunion attracted 67 graduates, while our 30-year reunion attracted 41 graduates.

_____ 17. When I came downstairs for breakfast, I saw an **incongruous** sight:
- A. Someone had set the table and made fresh coffee.
- B. All the plates and silverware from dinner were still on the counter, waiting to be washed.
- C. Our cat, normally afraid of water, was curled up in the kitchen sink.
- D. My brother was stirring a pot of oatmeal, which he makes every morning.

_____ 18. “Let me tell you about my **plight**,” the stranger said. “You see,
- A. I’ve left my wallet in a taxi and I have no money to get home.”
- B. I was born in Kansas and my parents were farmers.”
- C. I collect rare stamps and coins.”
- D. I’d like to offer you a tremendous opportunity to make money.”

_____ 19. Tamika is interested only in **sedentary** jobs, such as
- A. digging ditches.
- B. working in a busy sporting-goods store.
- C. teaching physical-education classes.
- D. sitting at a desk answering an office phone.

_____ 20. Some people wanted the fired teacher to be **reinstated** because she
- A. didn’t deserve her pension.
- B. had already started working at a new job.
- C. was an excellent teacher.
- D. had allowed cheating in her classroom.

Score (Number correct) _________ x 5 = _________%

Enter your score above and in the **Vocabulary Performance Chart** on the inside back cover of the book.

UNIT TWO: Test 2

PART A

Complete each item with a word from the box. Use each word once.

A. **circumvent**	B. **conspiracy**	C. **contrite**	D. **exonerate**	E. **facsimile**
F. **grievous**	G. **inundate**	H. **lucid**	I. **metamorphosis**	J. **oblivious**
K. **prolific**	L. **tenet**	M. **vociferous**		

________________ 1. After Cristina learned to read at age 30, she underwent a(n) ___. She changed from being shy to being confident, got an interesting new job, and started taking college classes at night.

________________ 2. According to *Guinness World Records*, the most ___ woman on record is a Russian peasant who lived in the early 1700s. She gave birth to sixty-nine children—sixteen pairs of twins, seven sets of triplets, and four sets of quadruplets.

________________ 3. The dictator arrested everyone involved in the ___ to overthrow him, including his wife.

________________ 4. A(n) ___ of a medical record isn't official unless it has been stamped with the doctor's signature.

________________ 5. The boys were ___ when they realized that their teasing had made Mary afraid to go to school the next day.

________________ 6. We tried to ___ the construction area by taking the other highway, but that road was being repaired too.

________________ 7. The main ___ of the "Girls Are Great" club is that girls can do anything boys can do.

________________ 8. Gerry was accused of stealing a wallet but was ___(e)d when the wallet was found in another student's locker.

________________ 9. Susan signed in and began work, ___ to the fact that she had forgotten to change from her bedroom slippers into her shoes.

________________ 10. After telling a reader to say goodbye to her boyfriend, the newspaper advice columnist was ___(e)d with thousands of letters saying she was wrong.

________________ 11. When three-year-old Ginger doesn't get what she wants, her protests are so ___ that you can hear her all over the neighborhood.

________________ 12. People who ignore their elderly parents do them a(n) ___ wrong.

________________ 13. Correct punctuation makes prose more ___.

(Continues on next page)

PART B

Write **C** if the italicized word is used **correctly**. Write **I** if the word is used **incorrectly**.

____ 14. Doris calls herself *inquisitive* because she likes to ask people so many questions, but personally, I think she's just plain nosy.

____ 15. The yearbook meeting got sidetracked. Our discussion of our instructors' merits and flaws wasn't *germane* to the topic of the photo layout.

____ 16. Rose's "How are you?" always seems *perfunctory*, just a matter of routine courtesy, not genuine interest.

____ 17. Marsha, as *verbose* as always, signed her letter only "Best," instead of "Best wishes."

____ 18. Our bodies are perfectly *symmetrical*—one side is always bigger than the other.

____ 19. Alan is saving his old comic books, hoping they will *depreciate* in value so he can sell them for a profit.

____ 20. My cousin is so *egocentric* that when the family got together for his sister's graduation, the only pictures he took were of himself.

____ 21. The science museum has many *provocative* exhibits, including a giant heart that visitors can walk through.

____ 22. Frannie's conversation is so *nebulous* that I always know exactly what she thinks and feels about a subject.

____ 23. A tall tree *indigenous* to Australia has been successfully transplanted to the edge of the Sahara Desert, where it keeps the desert from spreading.

____ 24. I was *distraught* when I got the raise I had asked for.

____ 25. My uncle is quite *terse*. He talks for at least an hour every time I call him.

Score (Number correct) ________ x 4 = ________%

Enter your score above and in the **Vocabulary Performance Chart** on the inside back cover of the book.

UNIT TWO: Test 3

PART A: Synonyms

In the space provided, write the letter of the choice that is most nearly the **same** in meaning as the **boldfaced** word.

____ 1. **travesty** A. long journey B. complete change C. ridiculous imitation D. disapproval

____ 2. **germane** A. well-known B. troubled C. distorted D. relevant

____ 3. **facsimile** A. proof B. copy C. disadvantage D. something unusual

____ 4. **relegate** A. send to a worse place B. delay C. promote D. leave

____ 5. **egocentric** A. self-confident B. self-taught C. self-centered D. selfless

____ 6. **bolster** A. question B. support C. fix D. allow

____ 7. **prolific** A. successful B. healthy C. fertile D. clear

____ 8. **notorious** A. heroic B. ill-famed C. vague D. unaware

____ 9. **conspiracy** A. know-how B. reproduction C. dilemma D. plot

____ 10. **metamorphosis** A. possibility B. puzzle C. change D. loss

____ 11. **depreciate** A. break down B. forget C. grow D. fall in value

____ 12. **inundate** A. flood B. protect C. visit D. hypnotize

____ 13. **contingency** A. event B. possibility C. plan D. disadvantage

____ 14. **reinstate** A. restore B. find C. state again D. select

____ 15. **inquisitive** A. unnecessary B. hard-working C. questioning D. difficult

____ 16. **mesmerize** A. explain B. permit C. confuse D. fascinate

____ 17. **circumvent** A. avoid B. delay C. repeat D. face

____ 18. **perfunctory** A. creative B. routine C. careful D. perfect

____ 19. **attrition** A. health B. permission C. shrinkage D. addition

____ 20. **provocative** A. illegal B. interesting C. lawful D. careless in choosing

____ 21. **vociferous** A. unaware B. noisy C. serious D. native

____ 22. **replete** A. full B. supported C. plain D. quiet

____ 23. **tenet** A. aid B. principle C. boarder D. drawback

____ 24. **terse** A. organized B. quiet C. interesting D. concise

____ 25. **plight** A. difficulty B. future C. plot D. aid

(Continues on next page)

PART B: Antonyms

In the space provided, write the letter of the choice that is most nearly the **opposite** in meaning to the **boldfaced** word.

____ 26. **verbose** A. correct B. concise C. confident D. cautious

____ 27. **clandestine** A. legal B. weak C. peaceful D. out in the open

____ 28. **liability** A. amusement B. praise C. response D. advantage

____ 29. **connoisseur** A. follower B. leader C. beginner D. expert

____ 30. **oblivious** A. helpful B. aware C. talkative D. unselfish

____ 31. **distraught** A. calm B. factual C. innocent D. unknown

____ 32. **grievous** A. pleasing B. famous C. choosy D. careless

____ 33. **exonerate** A. admire B. prove guilty C. harm D. support

____ 34. **contrite** A. ambitious B. misinformed C. not sorry D. lacking curiosity

____ 35. **robust** A. lazy B. dull C. hungry D. weak

____ 36. **lucid** A. secret B. shy C. inactive D. unclear

____ 37. **superfluous** A. expensive B. common C. necessary D. plain

____ 38. **superficially** A. carefully B. cheaply C. lately D. easily

____ 39. **nebulous** A. near B. clever C. clear D. troubled

____ 40. **austere** A. loud B. luxurious C. disorganized D. important

____ 41. **indiscriminate** A. lucky B. helpful C. choosy D. efficient

____ 42. **esoteric** A. famous B. unnecessary C. inexpensive D. widely understood

____ 43. **sedentary** A. helpful B. expert C. active D. loud

____ 44. **sanction** A. dislike B. prohibit C. lower in value D. avoid

____ 45. **reticent** A. happy B. talkative C. loyal D. having a good reputation

____ 46. **incongruous** A. likely B. consistent C. serious D. quiet

____ 47. **cohesive** A. routine B. coming apart C. sticking together D. not enough

____ 48. **indigenous** A. rich B. poor C. foreign D. legal

____ 49. **grotesque** A. well-formed B. caring C. fancy D. uninterested

____ 50. **symmetrical** A. irrelevant B. dull C. unbalanced D. ugly

Score (Number correct) ________ x 2 = ________%

Enter your score above and in the **Vocabulary Performance Chart** on the inside back cover of the book.

UNIT TWO: Test 4

Each item below starts with a pair of words in CAPITAL LETTERS. For each item, figure out the relationship between these two words. Then decide which of the choices (A, B, C, or D) expresses a similar relationship. Write the letter of your choice on the answer line.

____ 1. CONTINGENCY : PREPARE ::
A. accident : happen
B. car : repair
C. mistake : intend
D. goal : aim

____ 2. EXONERATE : EVIDENCE ::
A. pollute : chemicals
B. bake : cake
C. write : essay
D. sleep : energy

____ 3. RETICENT : SILENT ::
A. evil : ugly
B. lighthearted : gloomy
C. helpful : nurse
D. well-known : famous

____ 4. VOCIFEROUS : PROTESTORS ::
A. violent : peace-lovers
B. brave : heroes
C. virtuous : criminals
D. victorious : losers

____ 5. BOLSTER : WEAKEN ::
A. heal : cure
B. scrub : clean
C. build : destroy
D. search : hope

____ 6. INDISCRIMINATE : SELECTIVE ::
A. indistinct : vague
B. injurious : harmful
C. content : satisfied
D. intolerant : open-minded

____ 7. SEDENTARY : RECEPTIONIST ::
A. healthy : plumber
B. hammer : carpenter
C. dangerous : firefighter
D. unskilled : nuclear physicist

____ 8. TENET : RELIGION ::
A. custom : culture
B. hobby : workplace
C. law : friendship
D. foreign policy : day-care center

____ 9. CIRCUMVENT : GO AROUND ::
A. circulate : stop
B. tunnel : go over
C. bridge : go back
D. depart : go away

____ 10. OBLIVIOUS : AWARE ::
A. obvious : clear
B. insulting : disrespectful
C. optional : required
D. unclear : vague

(Continues on next page)

____ 11. SUPERFICIALLY : UNDERSTAND ::
A. thoroughly : examine
B. slowly : read
C. briefly : visit
D. race : run

____ 12. SYMMETRICAL : SQUARE ::
A. boxy : circle
B. circular : rectangle
C. triangular : hoop
D. egg-shaped : oval

____ 13. AUSTERE : PLAIN ::
A. remote : control
B. nearby : close
C. strict : easygoing
D. selfish : tantrum

____ 14. ESOTERIC : BRAIN SURGERY ::
A. logical : infancy
B. daring : jogging
C. noisy : sleeping
D. challenging : mountain climbing

____ 15. FACSIMILE : ORIGINAL ::
A. parent : adult
B. reproduction : painting
C. brother : man
D. piano : pianist

____ 16. MESMERIZE : HYPNOTIST ::
A. operate : surgeon
B. listen : lecturer
C. disappear : announcer
D. repair : undertaker

____ 17. CONNOISSEUR : TASTE ::
A. computer programmer : height
B. proofreader : courage
C. comedian : wit
D. acrobat : clumsiness

____ 18. CONSPIRACY : PLOTTERS ::
A. football field : athletes
B. blueprint : architects
C. railroad : conductors
D. television : viewers

____ 19. INCONGRUOUS : BLUE APPLE ::
A. unbearable : comfortable
B. inferior : first-class
C. inedible : granite
D. impossible : somersault

____ 20. PROLIFIC : OFFSPRING ::
A. deceptive : truth
B. imaginative : ideas
C. children : parents
D. teacher : students

Score (Number correct) ________ x 5 = ________%

Enter your score above and in the **Vocabulary Performance Chart** on the inside back cover of the book.

Unit Three

Chapter 11

adept	presumptuous
encompass	sordid
entrepreneur	standardize
eradicate	stint
homogeneous	stringent

Chapter 12

exhort	masochist
flamboyant	meticulous
foible	rancor
innocuous	recrimination
magnanimous	repugnant

Chapter 13

atrophy	mitigate
deplore	objective
deprivation	panacea
exacerbate	unprecedented
imperative	utilitarian

Chapter 14

decorum	facilitate
espouse	orthodox
exhilaration	rejuvenate
exorbitant	synchronize
extricate	tenuous

Chapter 15

analogy	placebo
annihilate	proficient
criterion	staunch
emanate	subversive
holistic	vindicate

adept	presumptuous
encompass	sordid
entrepreneur	standardize
eradicate	stint
homogeneous	stringent

Ten Words in Context

In the space provided, write the letter of the meaning closest to that of each **boldfaced** word. Use the context of the sentences to help you figure out each word's meaning.

1 adept
(ə-dĕpt′)
-adjective

- People enjoy visiting my parents, who are **adept** at making guests feel welcome and at home.
- Justin is an **adept** liar. He always looks so innocent and sincere that everyone believes his lies.

___ *Adept* means A. skillful. B. profitable. C. awkward.

2 encompass
(ĕn-kŭm′pəs)
-verb

- Our history teacher's broad knowledge of the subject **encompasses** details of life in ancient Egypt, Greece, and India.
- Tomorrow's test will be difficult because it **encompasses** all the material covered this semester.

___ *Encompass* means A. to suggest. B. to omit. C. to include.

3 entrepreneur
(ŏn′trə-prə-nûr′)
-noun

- Glenville has no shopping center, but the city is growing so quickly that smart **entrepreneurs** are sure to start up new businesses there soon.
- My ten-year-old neighbor is already an **entrepreneur**. He set up a lemonade stand last summer and sold homemade cookies at Halloween.

___ *Entrepreneur* means A. a business investor. B. an overconfident person. C. a conformist.

4 eradicate
(ĭ-răd′ĭ-kāt′)
-verb

- In recent years, smallpox has been **eradicated**—the first time in history that humans have been able to wipe out a disease.
- What makes so many people feel they must **eradicate** all signs of aging? Why should we have to get rid of our wrinkles and gray hair?

___ *Eradicate* means A. to reveal. B. to regulate strictly. C. to erase.

5 homogeneous
(hō′mō-jē′nē-əs)
-adjective

- The student body at the local college appears quite **homogeneous**, but there are significant social and economic differences among the students.
- "Homogenized" milk has been made **homogeneous**. This means that it's treated so it will be of uniform consistency, rather than having the cream rise to the top.

___ *Homogeneous* means A. strictly controlled. B. the same throughout. C. of high quality.

6 presumptuous
(prē-zŭmp′cho͞o-əs)
-adjective

- It was **presumptuous** of Eric to announce his engagement to Phyllis before she had actually agreed to marry him.
- If you ask personal questions at a job interview, you'll be considered **presumptuous**. So, for example, don't ask the interviewer, "What are they paying you?"

___ *Presumptuous* means A. too forward. B. skilled. C. cautious.

7 sordid
(sôr′dĭd)
-adjective

- Celebrity gossip websites are popular because many people want to know the **sordid** details of celebrities' relationships and private lives.
- The reformed criminal now lectures at high schools on how to avoid the mistakes that led him into a **sordid** life as a drug dealer.

__ *Sordid* means A. proud. B. ugly. C. natural.

8 standardize
(stăn′dər-dīz′)
-verb

- When the company **standardized** its pay scale, the salary for each type of job became identical throughout all the departments.
- If Jamila begins selling her delicious homemade soup, she'll have to **standardize** the ingredients. Now she just puts in whatever she has on hand, so the soup is never the same from one day to the next.

__ *Standardize* means A. to do away with. B. to make the same. C. to vary.

9 stint
(stĭnt)
-noun

- My **stint** serving hamburgers and fries at a fast-food restaurant convinced me that I needed to get a college degree.
- After traveling during her **stint** in the Navy, Alise wanted a job that would let her continue to see the world.

__ *Stint* means A. a length of time. B. a risky undertaking. C. future work.

10 stringent
(strĭn′jənt)
-adjective

- Ms. Jasper has the most **stringent** standards in the English department. Passing her course is difficult; getting an A is next to impossible.
- Elected officials should be held to a **stringent** code of ethics, requiring them to avoid even the appearance of wrongdoing.

__ *Stringent* means A. different. B. flexible. C. demanding.

Matching Words with Definitions

Following are definitions of the ten words. Clearly write or print each word next to its definition. The sentences above and on the previous page will help you decide on the meaning of each word.

1. ______________ A person who organizes, manages, and takes the risk of a business undertaking
2. ______________ Highly skilled; expert
3. ______________ A specific period of work or service; amount of time spent
4. ______________ Too bold; overly confident
5. ______________ To get rid of altogether; wipe out
6. ______________ Strictly controlled or enforced; strict; severe
7. ______________ To make consistent; cause to conform to a model
8. ______________ To include; contain
9. ______________ Made up of similar or identical parts; unvarying throughout
10. ______________ Indecent; morally low; corrupt

CAUTION: Do not go any further until you are sure the above answers are correct. Then you can use the definitions to help you in the following practices. Your goal is eventually to know the words well enough so that you don't need to check the definitions at all.

Sentence Check 1

Using the answer line provided, complete each item below with the correct word from the box. Use each word once.

A. adept	B. encompass	C. entrepreneur	D. eradicate	E. homogeneous
F. presumptuous	G. sordid	H. standardize	I. stint	J. stringent

________ 1. Joyce and Steven's adopted son was neglected in an earlier home. They're working hard to ___ the lingering effects on him of that experience.

________ 2. My grandfather held many jobs during his life. He even did a(n) ___ as a circus performer.

________ 3. In the novel *Oliver Twist*, innocent young Oliver falls into the hands of a gang of pickpockets, who teach him their ___ trade.

________ 4. It takes years of study and practice to become ___ at acupuncture.

________ 5. It's ___ of Amy to assume she got the job when others are still being interviewed.

________ 6. Should the high-school curriculum be ___(e)d throughout the state? Or should each school district be free to design its own courses?

________ 7. Ramon has just opened an auto repair shop. Now that he's a(n) ___, he can join the National Association for the Self-Employed.

________ 8. My sister applied to several colleges, some with very high admission standards for their students and others with less ___ requirements.

________ 9. The articles in our small newspaper ___ local and statewide news, but not national or international events.

________ 10. The town is so close-knit and ___ that newcomers feel out of place. Many of the residents are even related to each other.

NOTE: Now check your answers to these items by turning to page 130. Going over the answers carefully will help you prepare for the next two practices, for which answers are not given.

Sentence Check 2

Using the answer lines provided, complete each item below with **two** words from the box. Use each word once.

____
________ 1–2. After serving a prison term for theft, Charlie is contrite°. He's decided to begin a new life as an honest citizen and ___ all traces of his ___ past.

____
________ 3–4. During Nate's ___ as a teacher at a military academy, he felt that the ___ rules hampered his easygoing, flexible approach.

____
________ 5–6. To succeed, ___s must be ___ at organization and management. In addition, they must be resilient° enough to deal with the ups and downs of running a business.

____
____

7–8. The instructors of the English as a Second Language class have finally ___(e)d their approach. At the first class, all students meet as a group and take a placement test. After that, they are divided into smaller, more ___ classes.

____
____

9–10. I've been working at the daycare center only one week, so this suggestion may be ___, but I think the center's program should ___ activities geared to shy children as well as ones for gregarious° kids.

Final Check: *An Ohio Girl in New York*

Here is a final opportunity for you to strengthen your knowledge of the ten words. First read the following selection carefully. Then fill in each blank with a word from the box at the top of the previous page. (Context clues will help you figure out which word goes in which blank.) Use each word once.

© kostastudio/shutterstock.com

Soon after Gina moved from her small Ohio town to New York City, she became so discouraged that she nearly returned home. It was easy to see why she was despondent°: New York had the glamour and excitement that she had expected, but not the high-paying jobs. However, Gina decided to stay in the big city and put in a(n) (1)_______________ as a waitress in a coffee shop while hoping for something better to turn up. She had been offered only one higher-paying job, calling senior citizens and trying to scare them into buying an expensive, unproven "anti-cancer pill," but she thought this kind of work was too (2)_______________.

At least she enjoyed the coffee shop. For someone used to a small, (3)_______________ town, the customers seemed to come in an enormous variety. Also, the low salary forced her to stick to a(n) (4)_______________ budget. As a result of her unsteady financial situation, she was becoming (5)_______________ at making one dollar go as far as two did before.

One day, Gina met a customer who had recently opened a furniture rental store. This (6)_______________ mentioned to her that he was about to open a second store. Although she worried that he might think it (7)_______________ of a waitress to offer a suggestion about the furniture business, Gina told him a thought she had about how he might (8)_______________ his rental system by using a website. She explained how customers could enter their information on the site, which would (9)_______________ renter data from both stores. This way, all customer records would be in one place and easier to access. To Gina's relief, the customer didn't scoff° at her idea; in fact, he thanked her for the advice.

Sometime later, he stopped in at the coffee shop to say he needed a capable person to manage his new store. He offered Gina the job. Within a year, she was the manager of three furniture rental stores and earning an excellent salary. She was euphoric°, but her happiness would never fully (10)_______________ her memories of those difficult first months in New York.

Scores Sentence Check 2 ________% Final Check ________%

Enter your scores above and in the **Vocabulary Performance Chart** on the inside back cover of the book.

exhort
flamboyant
foible
innocuous
magnanimous
masochist
meticulous
rancor
recrimination
repugnant

Ten Words in Context

In the space provided, write the letter of the meaning closest to that of each **boldfaced** word. Use the context of the sentences to help you figure out each word's meaning.

1 exhort
(ĕg-zôrt′)
-verb

- The school counselor gave an impassioned speech to the parents, in which she **exhorted** them to make every effort to keep their children off drugs.
- On the eve of the invasion, the general **exhorted** the troops to fight bravely for their homeland.

__ *Exhort* means A. to accuse. B. to praise. C. to urge.

2 flamboyant
(flăm-boi′ənt)
-adjective

- Lily can't resist **flamboyant** clothes. She'd wear a hot-pink dress with gold satin trim to a funeral.
- The **flamboyant** pianist always wore sequined suits and glittering jewelry when he sat down at his silver piano.

__ *Flamboyant* means A. flashy. B. self-centered. C. concerned with details.

3 foible
(foi′bəl)
-noun

- Serious character flaws, such as abusiveness, are hard to overlook, but **foibles**—such as drinking soup through a straw—can often be easily tolerated.
- "I accept my husband's **foible** of leaving clothes lying around," Kia remarked, "because it lets me be messy without feeling guilty."

__ *Foible* means A. a serious problem. B. a minor fault. C. a complaint.

4 innocuous
(ĭn-nŏk′yo͞o-əs)
-adjective

- Although most children engage in **innocuous** pranks on Halloween, some get out of control and do serious damage.
- Experts at the Poison Information Center can tell you if a household substance is harmful or **innocuous**.

__ *Innocuous* means A. without bad effects. B. expensive. C. satisfying.

5 magnanimous
(măg-năn′ə-məs)
-adjective

- At age five, Jonathan is already learning to be **magnanimous**. He hugs his baby sister, even when she hits him on the head with a wooden block.
- Last Thanksgiving, someone at work drew a funny picture of our boss as an enormous turkey. When the boss saw it, he was **magnanimous**—he laughed, said it was terrific, and even hung it up over his desk.

__ *Magnanimous* means A. forgiving. B. consistent. C. resentful.

6 masochist
(măs′ə-kĭst)
-noun

- Psychologists are trying to understand why **masochists** obtain satisfaction from suffering.
- "A **masochist's** idea of a good time," said the comedian, "is getting hit by a truck on the way home from having all his teeth pulled."

__ *Masochist* means A. someone filled with hatred. B. someone who enjoys being hurt. C. someone who enjoys hurting others.

7 meticulous
(mə-tĭk′yo͞o-ləs)
-adjective

- When you proofread your own writing, be **meticulous**—check every detail.
- Marcus is **meticulous** about his appearance. He never has a wrinkle in his clothing or a hair out of place.

__ *Meticulous* means A. very careful. B. bold. C. unconcerned.

8 rancor
(răng′kər)
-noun

- The **rancor** between my uncles has lasted for twenty years, ever since Uncle Dmitri married the woman to whom Uncle Sergei had proposed.
- When there is long-lasting **rancor** between divorced parents, their children may also start to share this bitterness.

__ *Rancor* means A. a minor fault. B. deep hostility. C. secrecy.

9 recrimination
(rĭ-krĭm′ə-nā′shən)
-noun

- The couple's session with the marriage counselor failed miserably; it began with the husband and wife hurling accusations at each other, and it never progressed beyond these **recriminations**.
- When Lainie's father and her teacher met to discuss Lainie's poor grades, they exchanged **recriminations**—each accused the other of not helping her do better.

__ *Recrimination* means A. an urgent plea. B. a detailed suggestion. C. an accusation in reply.

10 repugnant
(rĭ-pŭg′nənt)
-adjective

- The scent of a passenger's tuna and pickle sandwich filled the bus with a **repugnant** odor that made Lisette gag.
- A snake is **repugnant** to many people—"Slimy!" they say, shivering with distaste. However, snakes are not at all slimy, and most are harmless.

__ *Repugnant* means A. disgusting. B. amusing. C. remarkable.

Matching Words with Definitions

Following are definitions of the ten words. Clearly write or print each word next to its definition. The sentences above and on the previous page will help you decide on the meaning of each word.

1. ____________________ Intense hatred or ill will; long-lasting resentment
2. ____________________ Harmless; inoffensive
3. ____________________ Offensive; distasteful; repulsive
4. ____________________ A person who gains satisfaction from suffering physical or psychological pain
5. ____________________ Very showy; strikingly bold
6. ____________________ A minor weakness or character flaw; a minor fault in behavior
7. ____________________ An accusation made in response to an accuser; countercharge
8. ____________________ To urge with argument or strong advice; plead earnestly
9. ____________________ Noble in mind and spirit; especially generous in forgiving
10. ____________________ Extremely careful and exact; showing great attention to details

CAUTION: Do not go any further until you are sure the above answers are correct. Then you can use the definitions to help you in the following practices. Your goal is eventually to know the words well enough so that you don't need to check the definitions at all.

Sentence Check 1

Using the answer line provided, complete each item below with the correct word from the box. Use each word once.

A. **exhort**	B. **flamboyant**	C. **foible**	D. **innocuous**	E. **magnanimous**
F. **masochist**	G. **meticulous**	H. **rancor**	I. **recrimination**	J. **repugnant**

_______________ 1. Before the football game, the coach gave a fiery pep talk. He ___(e)d the players to fight for the honor of the team and the school.

_______________ 2. Although nail-biting is only a ___, it can become maddening to a companion who observes it day after day.

_______________ 3. Don't call Nia a ___ just because she's taking an upper-level math class; she honestly enjoys the work.

_______________ 4. It was ___ of the Greens to forgive the driver who ran over their dog.

_______________ 5. Why is it that bats seem so ___? Do we think a flying mouselike creature is distasteful, or do we associate bats with vampires?

_______________ 6. On New Year's Day in Philadelphia, string bands called "Mummers" strut their stuff in ___ costumes designed to outshine all other bands in the parade.

_______________ 7. Some jobs needn't be done in a(n) ___ way. For instance, why sweep every speck of dust off a floor that's only going to get dirty again in an hour?

_______________ 8. The angry neighbors traded ___s: "Your wild kids trampled all over my flower bed!" "Well, your crazy dog dug up my lawn!"

_______________ 9. The long-standing ___ between the two women finally came to an end when one of them fell and the other rushed over to help her.

_______________ 10. To an allergic person, foods that are normally ___, such as milk or wheat, can cause discomfort and even serious illness.

NOTE: Now check your answers to these items by turning to page 130. Going over the answers carefully will help you prepare for the next two practices, for which answers are not given.

Sentence Check 2

Using the answer lines provided, complete each item below with **two** words from the box. Use each word once.

____
_______________ 1–2. Many people find the thought of a ___ seeking out and enjoying suffering to be as ___ as the idea of causing someone else to suffer.

____
_______________ 3–4. In a small business, it's important never to instigate° quarrels or let ___ develop. People must learn to be ___ and forgive each other's errors.

____
_______________ 5–6. My second-grade teacher had stringent° standards. For one thing, she ___(e)d us to be ___ about our handwriting. "Dot every *i*," she would say, "and cross every *t*."

__________ __________ 7–8. When Martha put on a bright red beaded dress with huge rhinestone earrings, ___s flew back and forth between her and her sister. "You look ridiculous in that outfit," her sister said. "It's much too ___." Martha replied, "Well, *your* clothes are the most boring I've ever seen."

__________ __________ 9–10. Walter is certainly odd. Still, most of his ___s—like wearing bedroom slippers to work and leaving bags of pretzels all over the office—are so ___ that nobody really minds them.

Final Check: *How Neat Is Neat Enough?*

Here is a final opportunity for you to strengthen your knowledge of the ten words. First read the following selection carefully. Then fill in each blank with a word from the box at the top of the previous page. (Context clues will help you figure out which word goes in which blank.) Use each word once.

Experts say that the most ordinary matters sometimes create the biggest problems in a marriage. If one spouse is a slob and the other is (1)__________, there is bound to be trouble.

At first, newlyweds tend to be (2)__________, readily forgiving each other's (3)__________s. The wife says it's "sweet" that her husband made the bed while she was still in it and "cute" that he grabbed her plate to wash it when she picked up her sandwich to take a bite. "You're so helpful," she coos. And he manages a smile when she dumps her too-expensive, too-(4)__________ gold sequined dress in the middle of the bedroom floor. "We've sure got a high-priced, flashy rug," he jokes.

© Monkey Business Images/shutterstock.com

But the honeymoon ends, and the characteristics that once seemed (5)__________ start to be seriously annoying. He begins to think, "Since my housekeeping is so impeccable°, why isn't she picking up my good habits? Why must I wade through dirty pantyhose to reach the closet? Why is there spaghetti sauce on the kitchen ceiling fan again?" He (6)__________s her to make more of an effort and to stop treating him like her servant.

And she begins to wonder about him: Why does he insist on dusting the tops of the door frames when no one can see them? So what if she squeezes the toothpaste from the middle of the tube—why should he find that harmless habit so (7)__________? Maybe he's a (8)__________—why else would he be so happy down on his knees, scrubbing the bathroom floor with a toothbrush (one of the "old" ones that he replaced after using it for a week)?

Soon the accusations and (9)__________s start. She yells, "You're a zealot° for neatness—that's all you care about. You spend more time holding that vacuum cleaner than you spend holding me!" He responds, "If you weren't so sloppy, I'd hold you more often. As it is, I have to climb over a mountain of junk just to get near you!"

Eventually, as the two of them continue arguing with each other and berating° each other, their feelings of (10)__________ become so strong that a breakup is inevitable. It won't be long before another relationship—so to speak—bites the dust.

Scores Sentence Check 2 ________% Final Check ________%

Enter your scores above and in the **Vocabulary Performance Chart** on the inside back cover of the book.

atrophy	mitigate
deplore	objective
deprivation	panacea
exacerbate	unprecedented
imperative	utilitarian

Ten Words in Context

In the space provided, write the letter of the meaning closest to that of each **boldfaced** word. Use the context of the sentences to help you figure out each word's meaning.

1 atrophy
(ă′trə-fē)
-verb

- Since unused muscles **atrophy**, an arm or a leg that remains in a cast for some time becomes thinner.
- "If you watch any more of those mindless television programs," my father said, "your brain will **atrophy**."

__ *Atrophy* means A. to grow. B. to waste away. C. to cause pain.

2 deplore
(dĭ-plôr′)
-verb

- Bernie **deplored** his coworkers' habit of taking home paper clips, Scotch tape, pens, and stationery from the office, a practice he felt was dishonest.
- Many people **deplore** some of the content on the internet but feel they must tolerate it, because they disapprove just as strongly of censorship.

__ *Deplore* means A. to condemn. B. to ignore. C. to make worse.

3 deprivation
(dĕp′rə-vā′shən)
-noun

- Children who spend their early years in institutions where they receive no love may suffer throughout life from the effects of this **deprivation**.
- Weight-loss programs typically claim that their members experience no sense of **deprivation**. "You'll never be hungry!" they promise.

__ *Deprivation* means A. a deficiency. B. a feeling of disapproval. C. a strong desire.

4 exacerbate
(ĕg-zăs′ər-bāt′)
-verb

- Scratching a mosquito bite only makes it worse: the scraping **exacerbates** the itching and may even cause an infection.
- Instead of soothing the baby, the sound of the music box seemed only to **exacerbate** his crying.

__ *Exacerbate* means A. to find the cause of. B. to relieve. C. to make worse.

5 imperative
(ĭm-pĕr′ə-tĭv)
-adjective

- It is **imperative** that I renew my driver's license today—it expires at midnight.
- "It is **imperative** for this letter to reach Mr. Rivera tomorrow," the boss said, "so please send it by Express Mail."

__ *Imperative* means A. impossible. B. difficult. C. essential.

6 mitigate
(mĭt′ə-gāt′)
-verb

- The disabilities resulting from Mr. Dobbs's stroke were **mitigated** by physical therapy, but he still has difficulty using his right arm.
- Time usually **mitigates** the pain of a lost love. When Richard's girlfriend broke their engagement, he was miserable, but now the hurt is much less.

__ *Mitigate* means A. to relieve. B. to worsen. C. to reveal.

7 objective
(əb-jĕk′tĭv)
-adjective

- Scientists must strive to be totally **objective** in their observations and experiments, putting aside their personal wishes and expectations.
- All too often, we let our own prejudices prevent us from being **objective** in judging others.

___ *Objective* means A. personal. B. fair. C. persuasive.

8 panacea
(păn′ə-sē′ə)
-noun

- My aunt considers vitamins a **panacea**. She believes that they can cure everything from chapped lips to heart disease.
- Ravi thinks his troubles would be over if he just had plenty of money. But money isn't a **panacea**; it wouldn't solve all his problems.

___ *Panacea* means A. a belief. B. a basic necessity. C. a complete solution.

9 unprecedented
(ŭn-prĕs′ĭ-dĕn′tĭd)
-adjective

- The election of Barack Obama to the presidency was **unprecedented** in American history—he was the first African-American president.
- The spring concert was "standing room only." This was **unprecedented**, the first time in our school's history that the concert had been sold out.

___ *Unprecedented* means A. never happening before. B. unprejudiced. C. controversial.

10 utilitarian
(yo͞o-tĭl′ə-târ′ē-ən)
-adjective

- One difference between "arts" and "crafts" is that crafts tend to be more **utilitarian**. They are generally created to serve a specific purpose.
- I prefer **utilitarian** gifts, such as pots and pans, to gifts that are meant to be just ornamental or beautiful.

___ *Utilitarian* means A. unique. B. practical. C. inexpensive.

Matching Words with Definitions

Following are definitions of the ten words. Clearly write or print each word next to its definition. The sentences above and on the previous page will help you decide on the meaning of each word.

1. ______________ To aggravate (a situation or condition); make more severe
2. ______________ To make less severe or less intense; relieve
3. ______________ Being the first instance of something; never having occurred before
4. ______________ Something supposed to cure all diseases, evils, or difficulties; cure-all
5. ______________ To wear down, lose strength, or become weak, as from disuse, disease, or injury (said of a body part); to wither away
6. ______________ Lack or shortage of one or more basic necessities
7. ______________ Necessary; urgent
8. ______________ Not influenced by emotion or personal prejudice; based only on what can be observed
9. ______________ Made or intended for practical use; stressing usefulness over beauty or other considerations
10. ______________ To feel or express disapproval of

CAUTION: Do not go any further until you are sure the above answers are correct. Then you can use the definitions to help you in the following practices. Your goal is eventually to know the words well enough so that you don't need to check the definitions at all.

Sentence Check 1

Using the answer line provided, complete each item below with the correct word from the box. Use each word once.

A. **atrophy**	B. **deplore**	C. **deprivation**	D. **exacerbate**	E. **imperative**
F. **mitigate**	G. **objective**	H. **panacea**	I. **unprecedented**	J. **utilitarian**

_______________ 1. No one could ___ drinking and driving more than Lin; her son was killed by a drunk driver.

_______________ 2. American swimmer Michael Phelps is the most decorated Olympian of all time, having won 28 medals—an ___ achievement.

_______________ 3. First-aid instructions usually advise against moving an accident victim, because movement can ___ an injury.

_______________ 4. The last time I had a migraine headache, I tried draping a cold, wet cloth over my eyes to ___ the pain and nausea, but my symptoms only got worse.

_______________ 5. When families go camping and decide to spend a whole weekend without video games and TV, some kids think they are experiencing a great ___.

_______________ 6. In Burma, some women lengthen their necks by stretching them with copper coils. This practice damages the muscles, causing them to ___: they become thin and weak.

_______________ 7. When told that Ms. Thomas was in conference and could not be disturbed, the caller said urgently, "It's ___ that I speak to her. Her house is on fire."

_______________ 8. Our city has many different crime-related problems, but the mayor has only one solution to offer: more police officers on the streets. She believes an enlarged police force is a ___.

_______________ 9. If you find it difficult to be ___ about your own writing, try asking a classmate to read it and give you an unbiased opinion.

_______________ 10. Although an Academy Award is not meant to be ___, one winner uses his as a paperweight.

NOTE: Now check your answers to these items by turning to page 130. Going over the answers carefully will help you prepare for the next two practices, for which answers are not given.

Sentence Check 2

Using the answer lines provided, complete each item below with **two** words from the box. Use each word once.

____
_______________ 1–2. Many people are so opposed to change that they ___ as potentially harmful just about anything that is new and ___.

____
_______________ 3–4. Students in our high school organized a food drive to help ___ hunger among families who are suffering ___.

____
____

5–6. In deciding which over-the-counter medicine to take, it's important to use a(n) ___ approach. Choose a drug for the specific purpose it serves, and don't rely on any one drug as a ___.

____
____

7–8. If you want to be ___, it is ___ that you put aside your emotions and prejudices.

____
____

9–10. It's hard to know what treatment is optimum° for a sprained ankle. Walking on the ankle can ___ the injury, but if you don't walk on it for a long time, the muscles will start to ___.

Final Check: *Thomas Dooley*

Here is a final opportunity for you to strengthen your knowledge of the ten words. First read the following selection carefully. Then fill in each blank with a word from the box at the top of the previous page. (Context clues will help you figure out which word goes in which blank.) Use each word once.

In the 1950s, a young American doctor named Thomas Dooley arrived in Laos, in southeast Asia. He was shocked by the ubiquitous° sickness and poverty he found there. The people lived without plumbing or electricity, and they had no knowledge of health care or even of basic hygiene. For example, one boy with an infected leg had been told not to walk at all, which caused both of his legs to (1)______________________. The people's lack of knowledge was (2)______________________(e)d by superstitions and by a reliance on well-meaning traditional healers, who sometimes inadvertently° gave useless or harmful advice. They might, for example, recommend pig grease for a burn or treat a fracture by chanting. Dooley (3)______________________(e)d the terrible (4)______________________ he saw. He felt that it was (5)______________________ to help these communities learn about modern medicine—to help them apply (6)______________________ scientific knowledge—and equally essential for them to relinquish° their harmful superstitions. Dooley did not believe that modern medicine would be a (7)______________________ for every problem in Laos, nor did he expect to eradicate° all disease there, but he firmly believed that he could at least (8)______________________ the people's suffering.

Dooley's (9)______________________ approach to health care, based specifically on practical instruction, was (10)______________________: no one before him had tried to teach the communities how to care for themselves. Dooley believed that teaching was a central part of medical care, that it was useless to treat symptoms and allow the causes to continue. So, subsidized° by local governments, he set up hospitals and taught the rudimentary° principles of hygiene, nursing, and medical treatment.

Tom Dooley died at a tragically young age, but his work and the tenets° that guided it benefited countless people.

Scores Sentence Check 2 ________% Final Check ________%

Enter your scores above and in the **Vocabulary Performance Chart** on the inside back cover of the book.

decorum	facilitate
espouse	orthodox
exhilaration	rejuvenate
exorbitant	synchronize
extricate	tenuous

Ten Words in Context

In the space provided, write the letter of the meaning closest to that of each **boldfaced** word. Use the context of the sentences to help you figure out each word's meaning.

1 decorum
(dĭ-kô′rəm)
-noun

- **Decorum** demands that you send a thank-you note for all birthday gifts, even those you don't like or will never use.
- **Decorum** is important on social media. Since a future employer could be watching, you should avoid posting crude comments or embarrasing photos on your pages.

__ *Decorum* means A. a difficult situation. B. beauty. C. proper conduct.

2 espouse
(ĕ-spouz′)
-verb

- Some politicians **espouse** whatever ideas they think will win them votes.
- People who **espouse** animals' rights often find themselves in conflict with scientists who argue for the use of animals in medical experiments.

__ *Espouse* means A. to speak for. B. to argue against. C. to study.

3 exhilaration
(ĕg-zĭl′ə-rā′shən)
-noun

- After the last exam of the year, Olivia and I were so filled with **exhilaration** that we skipped all the way to the car.
- A marching band gives most people a feeling of **exhilaration**. The lively music makes them feel excited.

__ *Exhilaration* means A. appropriateness. B. happiness. C. commitment.

4 exorbitant
(ĕg-zôr′bĭ-tənt)
-adjective

- Even if I were rich, I wouldn't pay three hundred dollars for those shoes. That's an **exorbitant** price.
- Critics of government spending often point to **exorbitant** amounts wasted on minor items, such as a toilet seat that cost six hundred dollars.

__ *Exorbitant* means A. estimated. B. inconvenient. C. extremely high.

5 extricate
(ĕks′trĭ-kāt′)
-verb

- The fly struggled and struggled but was unable to **extricate** itself from the spider's web.
- The young couple ran up so many debts that they finally needed a counselor to help them **extricate** themselves from their financial mess.

__ *Extricate* means A. to untangle. B. to distinguish. C. to excuse.

6 facilitate
(fə-sĭl′ə-tāt′)
-verb

- Automatic doors in supermarkets **facilitate** the entry and exit of customers with bags or shopping carts.
- For those with poor eyesight, large print **facilitates** reading.

__ *Facilitate* means A. to decrease. B. to cause. C. to make possible.

7 orthodox
(ôr′thə-dŏks′)
-adjective

- When Father McKenzie brought drums and electric guitars into church, he shocked the more **orthodox** members of his congregation.
- The **orthodox** footwear for a sprint or distance race is some kind of running shoes, but a champion Ethiopian runner competed in the Olympics barefoot.

__ *Orthodox* means A. revolutionary. B. traditional. C. important.

8 rejuvenate
(rĭ-jo͞o′və-nāt′)
-verb

- The Fountain of Youth was a legendary spring whose water could **rejuvenate** people.
- The grass had become brown and matted, but a warm spring rain **rejuvenated** it, perking it up and turning it green again.

__ *Rejuvenate* means A. to set free. B. to excite. C. to give new life to.

9 synchronize
(sĭng′krə-nīz′)
-verb

- The secret agents **synchronized** their watches so that they could cross the border at exactly the same minute.
- We need to **synchronize** the clocks in our house: the kitchen clock is ten minutes slower than the alarm clock in the bedroom.

__ *Synchronize* means A. to coordinate. B. to repair. C. to find.

10 tenuous
(tĕn′yo͞o-əs)
-adjective

- It doesn't take much to destroy an already **tenuous** relationship. Something as slight as forgetting to telephone can cause an unstable relationship to collapse.
- Del was opposed to the Equal Rights Amendment, but his position seemed **tenuous**. He couldn't support it with any facts, and his logic was weak.

__ *Tenuous* means A. shaky. B. easy. C. established.

Matching Words with Definitions

Following are definitions of the ten words. Clearly write or print each word next to its definition. The sentences above and on the previous page will help you decide on the meaning of each word.

1. ____________________ Cheerfulness; high spirits
2. ____________________ To free from a tangled situation or a difficulty
3. ____________________ Having little substance or basis; weak; poorly supported
4. ____________________ Correctness in behavior and manners; standards or conventions of socially acceptable behavior
5. ____________________ To make (someone) feel or seem young again; to make (something) seem fresh or new again
6. ____________________ To support, argue for, or adopt (an idea or cause)
7. ____________________ To cause to occur at exactly the same time; to cause (clocks and watches) to agree in time
8. ____________________ To make easier to do or to get
9. ____________________ Following established, traditional rules or beliefs, especially in religion; following what is customary or commonly accepted
10. ____________________ Excessive, especially in amount, cost, or price; beyond what is reasonable or appropriate

CAUTION: Do not go any further until you are sure the above answers are correct. Then you can use the definitions to help you in the following practices. Your goal is eventually to know the words well enough so that you don't need to check the definitions at all.

Sentence Check 1

Using the answer line provided, complete each item below with the correct word from the box. Use each word once.

A. **decorum**	B. **espouse**	C. **exhilaration**	D. **exorbitant**	E. **extricate**
F. **facilitate**	G. **orthodox**	H. **rejuvenate**	I. **synchronize**	J. **tenuous**

________ 1. The children's ___ at the amusement park was contagious—their parents soon felt excited too.

________ 2. The new restaurant went out of business because of its ___ prices.

________ 3. The ads for the anti-wrinkle cream claim that it will ___ aging skin.

________ 4. Some premature babies are so tiny and weak that their hold on life is very ___.

________ 5. Ignoring all standards of cafeteria ___, students sat on the tables and threw french fries at each other.

________ 6. "The ___ treatment in this kind of case," the doctor said, "is surgery followed by chemotherapy. But some specialists are exploring the possibility of using surgery alone."

________ 7. New members of the water ballet club have trouble coordinating their swimming, but with practice, the group is able to ___ its movements.

________ 8. During the 1960s and 1970s, there were bitter clashes between those who ___(e)d the United States' involvement in Vietnam and those who were opposed to it.

________ 9. At age two, Carlos got his head stuck between the bars of an iron railing. His parents had to call the fire department to come and ___ him.

________ 10. If you're giving a dinner party, preparing some food platters ahead of time will ___ your work when the guests arrive.

NOTE: Now check your answers to these items by turning to page 130. Going over the answers carefully will help you prepare for the next two practices, for which answers are not given.

Sentence Check 2

Using the answer lines provided, complete each item below with **two** words from the box. Use each word once.

____
________ 1–2. Although the price may seem ___, an expensive vacation may be worth the money, as it can often ___ one's mind and body.

____
________ 3–4. In any religion, ___ practices are slow to change. New ones are always in a(n) ___ position at first and require time to become widely accepted.

____
________ 5–6. It filled the audience with ___ to see the dexterous° dancers in the chorus line ___ their turns and kicks so perfectly.

____
____

7–8. My grandmother ___(e)d garlic as a treatment for chest colds, in the belief that it ___(e)d breathing. Sometimes she made us eat it, and sometimes she rubbed it on our chests. As a result, we were often excluded by our friends, who found the smell of garlic repugnant°.

____
____

9–10. Foreign Service officers must observe strict rules of conduct. If their behavior violates ___, their government may have to ___ itself from a diplomatic mess.

Final Check: *The Girl Who Fell from the Sky*

Here is a final opportunity for you to strengthen your knowledge of the ten words. First read the following selection carefully. Then fill in each blank with a word from the box at the top of the previous page. (Context clues will help you figure out which word goes in which blank.) Use each word once.

© Pablo Hidalgo/123rf

Peru, 1971. It was supposed to be a short flight. Seventeen-year-old Juliane had (1)________________(e)d schedules with her mother so the two would fly home together on Christmas Eve. However, any (2)________________ Juliane felt about going home for the holiday wouldn't last.

Before takeoff, Juliane's mother expressed that she didn't like flying. She (3)________________(e)d the belief that it was unnatural for a machine made of metal to fly like a bird. Still, their trip started off like a typical, (4)________________ flight. Sandwiches and drinks were served, which helped (5)________________ the passengers, who had waited in long lines to board the plane. But thirty minutes later, all (6)________________ was lost as the plane flew directly into a severe thunderstorm.

High winds slammed against the aircraft. Ubiquitous° lightning flashed on all sides in the darkening sky. Then Juliane noticed a flickering glow on the right wing. The motor had been struck, and the plane started to dive. Juliane's mother was convinced that their (7)________________ grip on life was ending and said, "Now it's over." Those were the last words Juliane heard her mother speak.

Clothes, suitcases, and wrapped presents, likely worth (8)________________ amounts of money, bounced around the falling airplane like cheap toys. Then Juliane herself was tumbling. The small plane had broken apart at 10,000 feet. Still belted to her seat, Juliane fell to the earth into a dense canopy of trees that miraculously cushioned her fall.

Hours later she woke up with relatively minor injuries and realized her grievous° plight°. After she (9)________________(e)d herself from the ruins of her seat, Juliane began an eleven-day trek through the dense rainforest before finally being rescued. Her survival was (10)________________(e)d by luck, determination, and knowledge she learned as a child about the rainforest near her home.

Juliane was the only survivor of the doomed flight.

Scores Sentence Check 2 _______% Final Check _______%

Enter your scores above and in the **Vocabulary Performance Chart** on the inside back cover of the book.

analogy	placebo
annihilate	proficient
criterion	staunch
emanate	subversive
holistic	vindicate

Ten Words in Context

In the space provided, write the letter of the meaning closest to that of each **boldfaced** word. Use the context of the sentences to help you figure out each word's meaning.

1 analogy
(ə-năl′ə-jē)
-noun

- To help students understand vision, teachers often draw an **analogy** between the eye and a camera.
- The commencement address, titled "You Are the Captain of Your Ship," used the **analogy** of life as an ocean-going vessel that the captain must steer between rocks.

__ *Analogy* means A. a picture. B. a comparison. C. a standard.

2 annihilate
(ə-nī′ə-lāt′)
-verb

- The movie was about a plot to **annihilate** entire cities by poisoning their water supply.
- "Universal Destroyer" is a warlike video game in which the aim is to **annihilate** the opponents.

__ *Annihilate* means A. to escape from. B. to seize. C. to wipe out.

3 criterion
(krī-tēr′ē-ən)
-noun

- One **criterion** by which writing teachers judge a paper is clear organization.
- Some advertisers aren't concerned about telling the truth. Their only **criterion** for a good commercial is selling the product.

__ *Criterion* means A. a standard. B. a beginning. C. an answer.

4 emanate
(ĕm′ə-nāt′)
-verb

- As the cinnamon bread baked, a wonderful smell **emanated** from the kitchen.
- The screeching and scraping **emanating** from Keisha's bedroom tell me that she is practicing her violin.

__ *Emanate* means A. to disappear. B. to come out. C. to expand.

5 holistic
(hō-lĭs′tĭk)
-adjective

- A good drug rehab takes a **holistic** approach to treatment, seeing each client not just as "an addict" but as a whole person. Along with medical aid, it provides emotional support, individual and family counseling, and follow-up services.
- Eastern cultures tend to take a more **holistic** view of learning than Western societies, focusing on the whole rather than analyzing parts.

__ *Holistic* means A. easygoing. B. concerned with the whole. C. nonfinancial.

6 placebo
(plə-sē′bō)
-noun

- When the little boy had a headache and there was no aspirin in the house, his mother gave him a **placebo**: a small candy that she told him was a "pain pill." It seemed to work—his headache went away.
- The doctor lost his license when it was found that the pills for depression he had been giving to many of his patients were actually a **placebo**—just sugar pills.

__ *Placebo* means A. a fake medicine. B. an over-the-counter pill. C. an expensive cure.

7 proficient
(prə-fĭsh′ənt)
-adjective

- It's not all that hard to become **proficient** at knitting. Watch instructional videos, be patient, and keep practicing to develop the skills.
- Wayne is a **proficient** woodworker. He is able to make professional-quality desks, bookshelves, and cabinets.

__ *Proficient* means A. expert. B. hard-working. C. enthusiastic.

8 staunch
(stônch)
-adjective

- Despite losing the first four games of the season, the city's football team still has legions of **staunch** fans who crowd the stadium to cheer on their squad.
- The newspaper's astrological predictions are often way off the mark, yet Teresa remains a **staunch** believer in astrology and checks her horoscope every day.

__ *Staunch* means A. busy. B. unsteady. C. faithful.

9 subversive
(səb-vûr′sĭv)
-adjective

- To some Americans, criticizing the president is a **subversive** act, aimed at undermining his power. To others, it is simply an example of freedom of speech.
- The so-called "consulting company" was a cover for **subversive** activities; it was actually a ring of antigovernment agents.

__ *Subversive* means A. having faith. B. intended to destroy. C. blameless.

10 vindicate
(vĭn′də-kāt′)
-verb

- When Kai was accused of cheating on a geometry test, he **vindicated** himself by reciting several theorems from memory, proving that he knew the material.
- In our society, people falsely accused of crimes often must spend a great deal of money on legal fees in order to **vindicate** themselves.

__ *Vindicate* means A. to prove innocent. B. to make a commitment. C. to weaken.

Matching Words with Definitions

Following are definitions of the ten words. Clearly write or print each word next to its definition. The sentences above and on the previous page will help you decide on the meaning of each word.

1. ______________________ To clear from blame or suspicion; justify or prove right
2. ______________________ A substance which contains no medicine, but which the receiver believes is a medicine
3. ______________________ To flow or come out from a source; come forth
4. ______________________ A comparison between two things in order to clarify or dramatize a point
5. ______________________ To destroy completely; reduce to nothingness
6. ______________________ A standard by which something is or can be judged
7. ______________________ Acting or intending to undermine or overthrow something established
8. ______________________ Firm; loyal; strong in support
9. ______________________ Emphasizing the whole and the interdependence of its parts, rather than the parts separately
10. ______________________ Skilled; highly competent

CAUTION: Do not go any further until you are sure the above answers are correct. Then you can use the definitions to help you in the following practices. Your goal is eventually to know the words well enough so that you don't need to check the definitions at all.

Sentence Check 1

Using the answer line provided, complete each item below with the correct word from the box. Use each word once.

A. **analogy**	B. **annihilate**	C. **criterion**	D. **emanate**	E. **holistic**
F. **placebo**	G. **proficient**	H. **staunch**	I. **subversive**	J. **vindicate**

____________ 1. Although I'm quite a good cook, I'm not very ___ at baking. My pies tend to be runny, and my bread won't rise.

____________ 2. One ___ used to judge the children's artwork was their use of vivid colors.

____________ 3. I'm a ___ fan of the writer J.K. Rowling. I have all her books.

____________ 4. Passenger pigeons no longer exist. They were ___(e)d by hunters.

____________ 5. During the Vietnam War, some protesters poured blood over draft records. Supporters of the war considered this a ___ act.

____________ 6. To test a new painkiller, researchers gave it to one group of volunteers, while a second group got a(n) ___, identical in appearance to the new medicine but with no built-in power to relieve pain.

____________ 7. Accused of shoplifting, the customer insisted that she had already paid for the items. She was ___(e)d when she pulled the receipt out of her purse.

____________ 8. Explaining the importance of using a search engine to find information on the internet, the instructor used a(n) ___. "The internet is a huge ocean. The search engine is a guide showing you the best places to fish."

____________ 9. As the garbage-collectors' strike went into its third week, a dreadful odor began to ___ from all the garbage bags piled up in the city streets.

____________ 10. A ___ view of business would take into account not just profits but also such things as the work environment and employees' job satisfaction.

NOTE: Now check your answers to these items by turning to page 130. Going over the answers carefully will help you prepare for the next two practices, for which answers are not given.

Sentence Check 2

Using the answer lines provided, complete each item below with **two** words from the box. Use each word once.

____
____________ 1–2. The agent was accused of selling government secrets, but he was able to ___ himself by proving that it was his boss who was the ___ one.

____
____________ 3–4. "One ___ by which I'll judge your papers," the teacher said, "is whether you are ___ at connecting your ideas into a cohesive° whole."

____
____________ 5–6. From the nasty smell that ___(e)d from the kitchen, I guessed that Mom was using a new kind of bug spray to try to ___ the ants there.

________________ ________________ 7–8. Anton is a ___ believer in the power of a(n) ___. When his small daughter started having nightmares about monsters, he sprayed the room with water and told her it was "anti-monster medicine."

________________ ________________ 9–10. To explain why she supported ___ medicine, the doctor used a(n) ___. She said that taking a narrow view of a health problem is like treating a dying tree's leaves but ignoring its roots, where the real problem lies.

Final Check: *A Different Kind of Doctor*

Here is a final opportunity for you to strengthen your knowledge of the ten words. First read the following selection carefully. Then fill in each blank with a word from the box at the top of the previous page. (Context clues will help you figure out which word goes in which blank.) Use each word once.

© Wong Yu Liang/123rf.com

Dr. Wilson considers (1)________________ medicine the optimum° approach to health care. He believes that to facilitate° healing and well-being, it is imperative° to consider a patient's entire lifestyle, not just specific aches and pains. To explain to patients how to keep well, he uses the (2)________________ of a garden. "If a garden gets too much or too little rain, sun, or fertilizer, it won't do well," he says. "But a proper balance keeps the garden healthy. In the same way, the body needs proper amounts of good food, exercise, work, and relaxation."

Dr. Wilson often treats patients without giving them drugs. Many of his patients have begun to feel healthier since they started taking his advice. They've adopted such new habits as eating more vegetables and taking a brisk walk every day. As a result, a new liveliness and an increased sense of pleasure and exhilaration° seem to (3)________________ from them; many say they feel rejuvenated°.

Despite Dr. Wilson's successes, many orthodox° physicians do not sanction° his methods, and some even deplore° them. They see him as dangerously (4)________________, a threat to the medical establishment; and they scoff° at his drug-free "prescriptions," calling them powerless (5)________________s. They fear he wants to (6)________________ medical progress.

Dr. Wilson, however, has no wish to destroy medical progress. To the contrary, he believes that his methods actually *are* progressive and that they are (7)________________(e)d by the improved health of his patients. There are other doctors worldwide who agree and who believe he is so (8)________________ at medicine that they often invite him to speak at professional conferences.

Dr. Wilson's patients also believe he is highly skilled, and they are the ones who are his most (9)________________ supporters. They judge him by a different (10)________________ from those who think medical progress lies only in finding new ways to treat disease. They judge him by the extent to which he helps his patients stay well.

Scores Sentence Check 2 ________% Final Check ________%

Enter your scores above and in the **Vocabulary Performance Chart** on the inside back cover of the book.

UNIT THREE: Review

The box at the right lists twenty-five words from Unit Three. Using the clues at the bottom of the page, fill in these words to complete the puzzle that follows.

adept
atrophy
decorum
emanate
encompass
exhort
extricate
foible
holistic
imperative
masochist
mitigate
objective
orthodox
panacea
placebo
rancor
rejuvenate
repugnant
sordid
staunch
stint
stringent
tenuous
vindicate

ACROSS

2. To clear from blame or suspicion; prove right
4. Intense hatred or resentment
6. Strictly controlled or enforced; strict; severe
7. A substance which contains no medicine, which the receiver believes is medicine
10. To free from a tangled situation or a difficulty
11. Indecent; corrupt
12. Necessary; urgent
21. Firm; loyal; strong in support
22. Not influenced by emotion or personal prejudice
23. A period of work or service
24. Offensive; repulsive

DOWN

1. A minor weakness or character flaw
3. Correctness in behavior and manners
5. Following established, traditional rules or beliefs, especially in religion
8. To wear down, lose strength, or become weak
9. Emphasizing the whole and the interdependence of its parts
10. To include; contain
13. A person who gains satisfaction from suffering pain
14. To urge with argument or strong advice; plead earnestly
15. Highly skilled; expert
16. To flow or come out from a source; come forth
17. To make (someone) feel or seem young again
18. Having little substance or basis; weak; poorly supported
19. To make less severe or less intense; relieve
20. Something supposed to cure all diseases or evils

UNIT THREE: Test 1

PART A

Choose the word that best completes each item and write it in the space provided.

______________ 1. It's amazing how I can ___ a thousand mosquitoes with bug spray, and an hour later another thousand appear.

A. espouse B. annihilate C. facilitate D. vindicate

______________ 2. Years ago, a shrewd ___ got the idea of selling "pet rocks" and made a fortune when they became a fad.

A. criterion B. analogy C. placebo D. entrepreneur

______________ 3. Even when textbooks are ___ throughout a school system, methods of teaching may vary greatly.

A. standardized B. emanated C. vindicated D. eradicated

______________ 4. Hang-gliding produces a feeling of ___ that few other activities can match.

A. exhilaration B. decorum C. criterion D. atrophy

______________ 5. Superstitious neighbors believe that a cold, clammy wind ___ from the "haunted" house on Elm Street.

A. synchronizes B. vindicates C. emanates D. mitigates

______________ 6. To ___ their movements so well, the dancers must practice doing the steps together for hours.

A. deplore B. extricate C. mitigate D. synchronize

______________ 7. Rules of ___ change over the years. For instance, my grandmother says that a lady always wears a hat to church, but few young women do so nowadays.

A. analogy B. decorum C. panacea D. placebo

______________ 8. In order to find a ring of spies trying to learn military secrets, the government agent pretended to be involved in ___ activities.

A. staunch B. tenuous C. holistic D. subversive

______________ 9. My ___ as a worker in the hotel laundry lasted only a day. It turned out that I was allergic to the soap.

A. placebo B. analogy C. foible D. stint

______________ 10. Working-class housing in nineteenth-century England was ___ by today's standards: crowded, dark, badly ventilated, and unsanitary.

A. innocuous B. meticulous C. sordid D. holistic

(Continues on next page)

PART B

On the answer line, write the letter of the choice that best completes each item.

____ 11. Commenting on the **exorbitant** prices in the restaurant, Willy said,
- A. "No wonder the restaurant is popular—it's such a bargain!"
- B. "The prices don't make sense—why is the lobster less expensive than the spaghetti?"
- C. "A cup of soup here costs more than a full meal anywhere else!"
- D. "Nothing is cheap, but nothing is very expensive either—the prices are reasonable."

____ 12. Because Ben and Susan had asked for **utilitarian** wedding gifts, a group of friends bought them
- A. whoopee cushions, rubber chickens, and fake spiders dangling from long threads.
- B. silk bedsheets, French champagne, and Russian caviar.
- C. a set of dishes and silverware.
- D. dozens of roses to decorate their apartment.

____ 13. Right after his heart attack, Alec's grip on life was so **tenuous** that his doctors
- A. did not expect him to live.
- B. admired his fighting spirit.
- C. were amazed at his quick recovery.
- D. realized the heart attack had been mild.

____ 14. When my boyfriend of two years dumped me, I wasn't surprised to hear my **staunch** friend say,
- A. "He wasn't good enough for you, anyway."
- B. "I don't want to hear about it."
- C. "Would you mind if I started dating him?"
- D. "It was probably your fault."

____ 15. Rita wears **flamboyant** hairstyles. Today, her hair is
- A. chin-length.
- B. in a ponytail.
- C. easily cared for.
- D. in green braids.

____ 16. When Annabelle broke off their engagement, Arthur showed he was **magnanimous** by saying,
- A. "How weird. I was just about to dump *you*."
- B. "You don't deserve me, and that's that."
- C. "I'm the unhappiest man in the world."
- D. "*Please* keep the three-carat diamond ring."

____ 17. When told he needed to have an operation, the **masochist**
- A. panicked, saying, "I just can't face that."
- B. wanted a second opinion.
- C. assumed that he would die.
- D. secretly hoped it would hurt quite a lot.

____ 18. It was **presumptuous** of my brother to
- A. volunteer his free time to work at a homeless shelter.
- B. refuse to lend money to his spendthrift pal Leon.
- C. call elderly, dignified Mr. Jackson "Larry" as soon as he met him.
- D. start giggling in the middle of a quiet church service.

____ 19. My mother considers chicken soup a **panacea**. According to her, it
- A. is the worst-tasting thing in the world.
- B. cures everything from flu to a broken heart.
- C. should be saved for special occasions.
- D. tastes good, but is not good for us.

____ 20. A truly **unprecedented** event would be
- A. an eclipse of the sun.
- B. the annual clearance sale at a sports store.
- C. the launching of a rocket into space.
- D. a TV interview with an alien life form.

Score (Number correct) ________ x 5 = ________%

Enter your score above and in the **Vocabulary Performance Chart** on the inside back cover of the book.

UNIT THREE: Test 2

PART A

Complete each item with a word from the box. Use each word once.

A. **atrophy**	B. **criterion**	C. **deplore**	D. **deprivation**	E. **eradicate**
F. **exhort**	G. **extricate**	H. **foible**	I. **objective**	J. **placebo**
K. **recrimination**	L. **rejuvenate**	M. **repugnant**		

________ 1. The two brothers will never make peace until they stop reacting to every accusation with another accusation. Such ___s only lead to more arguing.

________ 2. When little Sarah couldn't sleep, her mother gave her a ___ and called it a "magic sleeping potion." It was a glass of warm milk tinted light blue with food coloring.

________ 3. If the common cold were ever ___(e)d, it would be economically unhealthy for the makers of cold remedies.

________ 4. The TV preacher ___(e)d viewers to support his ministry with whatever funds they could manage to send.

________ 5. Judging people by their appearance makes it difficult to be ___ about their personalities.

________ 6. One ___ I use in selecting clothing is that an item be made out of a comfortable fabric.

________ 7. After Chrissy stayed awake studying for seventy-two hours, sleep ___ caused her to start having double vision and to hear voices that weren't there.

________ 8. The little boy's foot was so firmly caught in the folding chair that it took three adults to ___ him.

________ 9. My mother was feeling twice her age before her trip to Arizona, but the relaxing vacation really ___(e)d her.

________ 10. Although I ___ the conditions that face children born to drug addicts, I don't know what to do to help.

________ 11. The day after surgery, the nurses got Alonso out of bed and walking, so that his muscles would not begin to ___.

________ 12. The furry white and green mold growing on the old tomato sauce was a(n) ___ sight.

________ 13. One of my ___s is biting into many chocolates in a box until I find one I like.

(Continues on next page)

PART B

Write **C** if the italicized word is used **correctly**. Write **I** if the word is used **incorrectly**.

____ 14. As kids, my brother and I loved staying with our grandparents because of their *stringent* rules; they let us stay up as late as we liked and eat candy for breakfast.

____ 15. The nursery school teacher used the *analogy* of a flower garden to describe her class, saying that just as each flower has its own special beauty, so does each child.

____ 16. The load of oil dumped on the highway *facilitated* the flow of traffic for more than three hours.

____ 17. I didn't know that Jerry was so *proficient* in geography until I saw that F on his report card.

____ 18. Ricardo writes thoughtful essays and then spoils them by handing in a *meticulous* final draft filled with spelling and typing errors.

____ 19. It is *imperative* that my mother get her cholesterol level down, as she is now at high risk of a heart attack.

____ 20. Nadia's ankle injury is severe, but the doctor told her a couple of days of bed rest will *exacerbate* the sprain enough so that she can walk again.

____ 21. Lois and Manny were divorced three years ago, and they still feel such *rancor* that they refuse to speak to each other.

____ 22. It was bad enough being grounded, but my father is going to *mitigate* my punishment by stopping my allowance.

____ 23. The defendant, accused of murder, proclaimed his innocence and was *vindicated* when a man who looked just like him confessed.

____ 24. In an *orthodox* classroom, students' desks are lined up in rows.

____ 25. Only female black widow spiders are dangerous to humans. The bite of a male is *innocuous*.

Score (Number correct) ________ x 4 = ________%

Enter your score above and in the **Vocabulary Performance Chart** on the inside back cover of the book.

UNIT THREE: Test 3

PART A: Synonyms

In the space provided, write the letter of the choice that is most nearly the **same** in meaning as the **boldfaced** word.

____ 1. **utilitarian** A. showy B. spoken C. practical D. urgent

____ 2. **placebo** A. universal remedy B. peacefulness C. make-believe medicine D. disease

____ 3. **stint** A. standard B. lack C. work period D. businessperson

____ 4. **analogy** A. skill B. comparison C. lesson D. sermon

____ 5. **imperative** A. helpful B. beautiful C. essential D. reasonable

____ 6. **foible** A. imperfection B. goal C. personality characteristic D. skill

____ 7. **entrepreneur** A. politician B. boss C. business organizer and investor D. leader

____ 8. **decorum** A. blame B. correctness in manners C. flaw D. decoration

____ 9. **deprivation** A. dislike B. discipline C. necessity D. lack

____ 10. **holistic** A. all-inclusive B. partial C. healthy D. skillful

____ 11. **criterion** A. emotion B. insult C. standard D. habit

____ 12. **exhort** A. urge B. criticize C. agree D. oppose

____ 13. **emanate** A. delay B. come forth C. stay D. destroy

____ 14. **proficient** A. skilled B. innocent C. rebellious D. immoral

____ 15. **masochist** A. messy person B. servant C. actor D. one who welcomes pain

____ 16. **subversive** A. intended to overthrow B. supportive C. distasteful D. beneath

____ 17. **eradicate** A. blame B. break C. destroy D. dislike

____ 18. **extricate** A. advise B. make joyful C. rebel D. rescue

____ 19. **mitigate** A. ignore B. ease C. change D. worsen

____ 20. **presumptuous** A. unskilled B. bold C. timid D. skilled

____ 21. **standardize** A. destroy B. prove innocent C. make the same D. make worse

____ 22. **recrimination** A. countercharge B. just punishment C. second thoughts D. sadness

____ 23. **panacea** A. epidemic B. ill will C. support D. cure-all

____ 24. **synchronize** A. make happen together B. ease C. weaken D. urge

____ 25. **objective** A. bold B. based on facts C. shy D. based on emotions

(Continues on next page)

PART B: Antonyms

In the space provided, write the letter of the choice that is most nearly the **opposite** in meaning to the **boldfaced** word.

____ 26. **tenuous** A. relaxed B. reversed C. well supported D. partial

____ 27. **staunch** A. small B. unfaithful C. boring D. rich

____ 28. **atrophy** A. strengthen B. win C. support D. claim

____ 29. **meticulous** A. broken B. careless C. temporary D. unpopular

____ 30. **deplore** A. question B. provide C. approve of D. know of

____ 31. **exorbitant** A. legal B. high C. inexpensive D. happy

____ 32. **adept** A. unknown B. unskilled C. unpleasant D. unforgiving

____ 33. **magnanimous** A. physically small B. inexpensive C. perfect D. unforgiving

____ 34. **encompass** A. exclude B. get lost C. prevent D. do one at a time

____ 35. **exhilaration** A. weakness B. immorality C. sadness D. coming in

____ 36. **facilitate** A. make more difficult B. face C. disapprove of D. make older

____ 37. **sordid** A. talented B. colorful C. peaceful D. honorable

____ 38. **annihilate** A. approve of B. beautify C. create D. welcome

____ 39. **espouse** A. oppose B. participate C. ignore D. misrepresent

____ 40. **rancor** A. good manners B. goodwill C. good looks D. good luck

____ 41. **innocuous** A. all-inclusive B. too expensive C. harmful D. distasteful

____ 42. **exacerbate** A. come forth B. agree C. build D. improve

____ 43. **repugnant** A. pleasant B. wise C. important D. loyal

____ 44. **stringent** A. incorrect B. flexible C. caring D. usual

____ 45. **rejuvenate** A. disappoint B. blame C. make older D. cause to agree in time

____ 46. **homogeneous** A. varied B. similar C. wild D. ignorant

____ 47. **flamboyant** A. explosive B. cool C. dull D. cheap

____ 48. **orthodox** A. untraditional B. not required C. generous D. impractical

____ 49. **unprecedented** A. helpful B. moral C. strong D. common

____ 50. **vindicate** A. look back B. blame C. look forward D. help

Score (Number correct) ________ x 2 = ________%

Enter your score above and in the **Vocabulary Performance Chart** on the inside back cover of the book.

UNIT THREE: Test 4

Each item below starts with a pair of words in CAPITAL LETTERS. For each item, figure out the relationship between these two words. Then decide which of the choices (A, B, C, or D) expresses a similar relationship. Write the letter of your choice on the answer line.

____ 1. DEPLORE : SIN ::
A. praise : crime
B. foretell : predict
C. forget : forgiveness
D. seek : wisdom

____ 2. OBJECTIVE : JUDGE ::
A. treacherous : jury
B. sluggish : rock group
C. knowledgeable : teacher
D. obedient : parent

____ 3. ENTREPRENEUR : BUSINESS ::
A. dentist : patient
B. producer : movie
C. cook : fry
D. company : employee

____ 4. HOMOGENEOUS : SAME ::
A. juicy : cornflakes
B. fattening : celery
C. assorted : mixed
D. colorful : drab

____ 5. FLAMBOYANT : GRAY SUIT ::
A. economical : ten-course banquet
B. generous : thirty-percent tip
C. luxurious : palace
D. competitive : Olympics

____ 6. FOIBLE : NAIL-BITING ::
A. weakness : self-control
B. phobia : fear of heights
C. strength : compulsive gambling
D. skill : blue eyes

____ 7. MAGNANIMOUS : GENEROUS ::
A. angelic : heaven
B. softhearted : brutal
C. delicate : flower
D. affectionate : loving

____ 8. REPUGNANT : COCKROACHES ::
A. cheerful : ants
B. sturdy : butterflies
C. musical : songbirds
D. ruthless : doves

____ 9. ADEPT : PICKPOCKET ::
A. thin : chess player
B. scholarly : shortstop
C. graceful : dancer
D. cheerful : worrier

____ 10. ENCOMPASS : EXCLUDE ::
A. explain : clarify
B. insert : write
C. erase : remove
D. omit : include

(Continues on next page)

_____ 11. PLACEBO : SUGAR PILL ::
A. health : vitamins
B. prescription : subscription
C. leaf : lettuce
D. dwelling : igloo

_____ 12. PROFICIENT : INCAPABLE ::
A. talented : artistic
B. fake : genuine
C. immaculate : reputation
D. perceptive : observer

_____ 13. EXHILARATION : WALKING ON AIR ::
A. anxiety : being cool as a cucumber
B. weariness : being fresh as a daisy
C. ambitious : drifting along
D. depression : being down in the dumps

_____ 14. ESPOUSE : DENOUNCE ::
A. dislike : enemies
B. study : learn
C. complain : praise
D. distrust : doubt

_____ 15. FACILITATE : MAKE EASIER ::
A. postpone : delay
B. speak : speech
C. exaggerate : understate
D. fence : post

_____ 16. EXTRICATE : FREE ::
A. read : write
B. add : subtract
C. pledge : promise
D. ignore : celebrate

_____ 17. ANALOGY : COMPARISON ::
A. anatomy : music
B. anthology : collection
C. astronomy : medicine
D. anonymity : fame

_____ 18. HOLISTIC : WHOLE ::
A. skeptical : positive
B. physical : mental
C. fragmentary : part
D. weekly : monthly

_____ 19. UTILITARIAN : FRYING PAN ::
A. useless : doorway
B. electrical : water pipes
C. decorative : wallpaper
D. portable : foundation

_____ 20. UNPRECEDENTED : FAMILIAR ::
A. injurious : accidental
B. horrible : pleasant
C. abundant : plentiful
D. questioning : curious

Score (Number correct) ________ x 5 = ________%

Enter your score above and in the **Vocabulary Performance Chart** on the inside back cover of the book.

Unit Four

Chapter 16

disparity	obsequious
forestall	omnipotent
insidious	opportune
insinuate	permeate
interrogate	retribution

Chapter 17

complement	implement
discreet	impromptu
fastidious	inference
flout	intuition
heinous	obtrusive

Chapter 18

auspicious	rebuke
expedite	redeem
extenuating	subordinate
fraudulent	transgress
innuendo	vehement

Chapter 19

deride	misconstrue
derogatory	paramount
fabricate	quandary
impending	turbulent
macabre	validate

Chapter 20

abrasive	emulate
admonish	hierarchy
antithesis	incapacitate
culmination	prognosis
docile	tumult

disparity	obsequious
forestall	omnipotent
insidious	opportune
insinuate	permeate
interrogate	retribution

Ten Words in Context

In the space provided, write the letter of the meaning closest to that of each **boldfaced** word. Use the context of the sentences to help you figure out each word's meaning.

1 disparity
(dĭ-spăr′ə-tē)
-noun

- There's an enormous **disparity** between the multimillion-dollar incomes of top executives and the modest paychecks most people earn.
- Shirley and Jason don't let the **disparity** in their ages weaken their marriage, but Jason's mother isn't happy with a daughter-in-law her own age.

__ *Disparity* means A. a combination. B. a contrast. C. a closeness.

2 forestall
(fôr-stôl′)
-verb

- The owners of the failing store hoped that the huge sale would bring in enough cash to **forestall** bankruptcy.
- When the environmentalists were unable to **forestall** the destruction of the forest by legal means, they lay down in front of the developer's bulldozers.

__ *Forestall* means A. to keep from happening. B. to predict. C. to pay for.

3 insidious
(ĭn-sĭd′ē-əs)
-adjective

- Lyme disease is **insidious** because although it is very serious, it starts with a nearly invisible tick bite, and its early symptoms are mild.
- Many people fear that farm chemicals have **insidious** effects. The chemicals don't seem harmful, but cancer rates have started to increase.

__ *Insidious* means A. badly timed. B. subtly harmful. C. all-powerful.

4 insinuate
(ĭn-sĭn′yo͞o-āt′)
-verb

- He didn't come right out and say it, but Mr. Shriber **insinuated** that someone in the class had gotten hold of the test ahead of time.
- The police officer **insinuated** that I had been speeding when she said, "You certainly must be in a big hurry to get somewhere."

__ *Insinuate* means A. to hint. B. to wish. C. to state directly.

5 interrogate
(ĭn-tĕr′ə-gāt′)
-verb

- Before the police **interrogated** the suspect, they informed him of his right not to answer their questions.
- "You never just ask me if I had a nice time with my date," Tyrell complained to his parents. "Instead, you sit me down at the kitchen table and **interrogate** me."

__ *Interrogate* means A. to ask questions. B. to delay. C. to abuse.

6 obsequious
(ŏb-sē′kwē-əs)
-adjective

- Each of the queen's advisers tried to be more **obsequious** than the others, bowing as low as possible and uttering flowery compliments.
- Marge constantly flatters the boss, calls him "sir," and agrees loudly with everything he says. However, her **obsequious** behavior only annoys him.

__ *Obsequious* means A. unequal in rank. B. overly eager to please. C. methodical.

7 omnipotent
(ŏm-nĭp′ə-tənt)
-adjective

- Small children think of their parents as **omnipotent**—able to do anything, control everything, and grant whatever a child might wish for.
- The American government is designed so that no one branch can be **omnipotent**. Congress, the President, and the Supreme Court share power and hold each other in check.

__ *Omnipotent* means A. totally good. B. willing to serve. C. all-powerful.

8 opportune
(ŏp′ər-to͞on′)
-adjective

- Althea thought that her parents' anniversary would be an **opportune** time to announce her own engagement. They could have a double celebration.
- The job offer came at an especially **opportune** time. I had just decided that I might like to work for a year or so before returning to school.

__ *Opportune* means A. appropriate. B. difficult. C. early.

9 permeate
(pûr′mē-āt′)
-verb

- The strong scent of Kate's perfume soon **permeated** the entire room.
- The weather was so rainy and damp that moisture seemed to **permeate** everything: curtains hung limply, towels wouldn't dry, and windows were fogged over.

__ *Permeate* means A. to harm. B. to penetrate. C. to make unclear.

10 retribution
(rĕ′trə-byo͞o′shən)
-noun

- Some "sins" in life have their own built-in **retribution**. For example, if you get drunk, you'll have a hangover; if you overeat, you'll gain weight.
- For much of human history, before science could explain diseases, many people believed that any illness was a **retribution** for immoral behavior.

__ *Retribution* means A. an inequality. B. an obstacle. C. a penalty.

Matching Words with Definitions

Following are definitions of the ten words. Clearly write or print each word next to its definition. The sentences above and on the previous page will help you decide on the meaning of each word.

1. ____________________ Overly willing to serve, obey, or flatter in order to gain favor
2. ____________________ To suggest slyly
3. ____________________ Something given or done as repayment, reward, or (usually) punishment
4. ____________________ An inequality or difference, as in ages or amounts
5. ____________________ Working or spreading harmfully but in a manner hard to notice; more harmful than is evident at first
6. ____________________ To flow or spread throughout (something)
7. ____________________ Suitable (said of time); well-timed
8. ____________________ To prevent or hinder by taking action beforehand
9. ____________________ All-powerful; having unlimited power or authority
10. ____________________ To question formally and systematically

CAUTION: Do not go any further until you are sure the above answers are correct. Then you can use the definitions to help you in the following practices. Your goal is eventually to know the words well enough so that you don't need to check the definitions at all.

Sentence Check 1

Using the answer line provided, complete each item below with the correct word from the box. Use each word once.

A. **disparity**	B. **forestall**	C. **insidious**	D. **insinuate**	E. **interrogate**
F. **obsequious**	G. **omnipotent**	H. **opportune**	I. **permeate**	J. **retribution**

________ 1. When the Earl of Essex plotted against his queen, Elizabeth I of England, ___ was swift and harsh: she had him beheaded for treason.

________ 2. In many countries, political prisoners who are being ___(e)d by the secret police are likely to be tortured in an attempt to force answers from them.

________ 3. Because no one else's hand was raised, I considered it a(n) ___ moment to ask a question.

________ 4. To ___ complaints about unrepaired potholes, the township set up a "pothole hotline" and promised to fill in any reported hole within two days.

________ 5. When our dog was sprayed by a skunk, the smell soon ___(e)d the house.

________ 6. The headwaiter's manner toward customers who looked rich was ___. Ignoring the rest of us, he gave them the restaurant's best tables and hovered over them, all smiles.

________ 7. Instead of directly saying "Buy our product," many ads use slick images to ___ that the product will give the buyer popularity, power, or prestige.

________ 8. According to legend, King Canute—an ancient ruler of England, Denmark, and Norway—thought he was ___. He actually ordered the tide to stop rising.

________ 9. The effects of certain prescription drugs, such as Valium, can be ___. People who take them may slip into addiction without being aware of it.

________ 10. "There seems to be quite a ___," Shannon objected to the car dealer, "between your cost and the sticker price."

NOTE: Now check your answers to these items by turning to page 130. Going over the answers carefully will help you prepare for the next two practices, for which answers are not given.

Sentence Check 2

Using the answer lines provided, complete each item below with **two** words from the box. Use each word once.

____
________ 1–2. The toxic chemical spray used to eradicate° tentworms had ___ effects: after killing the worms, it gradually seeped down, ___(e)d the soil, and poisoned Duck Lake.

____
________ 3–4. The wide ___ between men's and women's pay in the company led to a protest by the women. The management tried to squelch° the protest and ___(e)d that the women were subversive° and were trying to ruin company morale.

______ ______ 5–6. In a job interview, use discretion°. Don't react as though you're being ___(e)d by the police; but don't be ___ either, as if the interviewer were a king or queen and you were a humble servant.

______ ______ 7–8. The remote control of my DVR makes me feel ___. I can ___ any pending disaster—a fire, a flood, an earthquake, a sordid° crime—by pressing a button and stopping the movie dead.

______ ______ 9–10. The ex-convict was filled with rancor°. As ___ for his years in prison, he planned to attack, at the first ___ moment, the judge who had sentenced him.

Final Check: *My Devilish Older Sister*

Here is a final opportunity for you to strengthen your knowledge of the ten words. First read the following selection carefully. Then fill in each blank with a word from the box at the top of the previous page. (Context clues will help you figure out which word goes in which blank.) Use each word once.

Anyone who thinks older sisters protect younger ones has never heard me tell about my sister Pam. There's no great (1)______ in our ages—Pam is only three years older—but throughout our childhood she was always able to beat me at cards, at jacks, at all board games. This seemingly unlimited power to win made me think of her as (2)______. I obeyed all her orders ("Relinquish° that lollipop!") and accepted all her insults ("You're grotesque°!" "You're positively repugnant°!") in the most timid, (3)______ manner. Privately, I longed for revenge.

© Andy Dean Photography/shutterstock.com

When Pam made up her mind to tease or trick me, there was nothing I could do to (4)______ her plans. And she never missed a(n) (5)______ moment to terrorize me. When our old dog growled, for no reason, at the empty air, she would (6)______ that evil spirits must have (7)______(e)d the atmosphere, saying, "Dogs, you know, can sense the supernatural." Once I made the mistake of revealing that crabs terrified me. After that, I was inundated° with photos of crabs, drawings of crabs, even labels from cans of crabmeat. In retrospect°, though, her most devious trick was giving me some "chocolate candy" that I impetuously° gobbled up. It turned out to be Ex-Lax. After that, if Pam offered me anything, no matter how innocuous° it looked, I always (8)______(e)d her: "What is it really? Do you still have the wrapping? Will you take a bite first?" But this episode also had a more (9)______ effect: for years, I was afraid of new foods.

Now that we're grown, Pam has greatly improved. She no longer likes to torment me, and she even seems contrite° about the past. However, I still sometimes think up various scenarios of (10)______ in which I am the older sister, and at last I get my revenge.

Scores Sentence Check 2 ______% Final Check ______%

Enter your scores above and in the **Vocabulary Performance Chart** on the inside back cover of the book.

complement	implement
discreet	impromptu
fastidious	inference
flout	intuition
heinous	obtrusive

Ten Words in Context

In the space provided, write the letter of the meaning closest to that of each **boldfaced** word. Use the context of the sentences to help you figure out each word's meaning.

1 complement
(kŏm′plə-mənt)
-verb

- The new singer's voice **complemented** the other voices, rounding out the group's sound.
- A red tie would **complement** Pedro's gray suit and white shirt, giving the outfit a needed touch of color.

__ *Complement* means A. to go perfectly with. B. to reach out for. C. to overpower.

2 discreet
(dĭ-skrēt′)
-adjective

- Once the teacher realized Jared could not read well, she made **discreet** efforts to give him extra help. She didn't want to embarrass him in front of his classmates.
- "Be **discreet** about these drawings, Wilson," the boss said. "Don't show them to just anyone. We don't want another company stealing our designs."

__ *Discreet* means A. honest. B. cautious. C. obvious.

3 fastidious
(făs-tĭd′ē-əs)
-adjective

- Tilly was a **fastidious** housekeeper who vacuumed every day, dusted twice a day, and never allowed so much as a pencil or safety pin to be out of place.
- A **fastidious** dresser, Mr. Lapp never leaves his home without looking as if he has just stepped out of a fashion magazine.

__ *Fastidious* means A. working quickly. B. having insight. C. very particular.

4 flout
(flout)
-verb

- My neighbors were evicted from their apartment because they **flouted** the building's rules. They threw trash in the hallway, had loud all-night parties, and just laughed at anyone who complained.
- The warehouse workers are **flouting** regulations about eating on the job. Wastebaskets are filled with sandwich wrappers and empty chip, pretzel, and nacho bags.

__ *Flout* means A. to mock and defy. B. to put into effect. C. to show off.

5 heinous
(hā′nəs)
-adjective

- Dracula is a famous literary villain known for the **heinous** act of drinking the blood of humans.
- Neighbors were shocked to learn of Mr. Sigby's **heinous** pastime: running a vicious dogfighting ring in his basement.

__ *Heinous* means A. wicked. B. unplanned. C. detailed.

6 implement
(ĭm′plə-mĕnt′)
-verb

- To keep the new carpet clean, my parents **implemented** a "no shoes indoors" rule.
- Brett is full of ideas about starting his own business, but he never follows through and **implements** them.

__ *Implement* means A. to recall. B. to put into effect. C. to criticize.

7 impromptu
(ĭm-prŏmp′too͞′)
-adjective

- My speech at my cousin's birthday dinner was **impromptu**; I hadn't expected to be called on to say anything.
- When Maya discovered that she and Barry had both brought guitars to the party, she suggested an **impromptu** duet.

__ *Impromptu* means A. not rehearsed. B. not very good. C. very quiet.

8 inference
(ĭn′fər-əns)
-noun

- Ruby said with a wink, "Did you notice how Uncle Joe's hair has miraculously grown back?" My **inference** was that he was wearing a toupee.
- "Where did you buy these pork chops?" asked Harry. "Why? What's wrong with them?" Maria asked, making the **inference** that he didn't like them.

__ *Inference* means A. a statement. B. a conclusion. C. a secret.

9 intuition
(ĭn′too͞-ĭsh′ən)
-noun

- "I paint by **intuition**," the artist said. "In a flash, I see how a work should look. I don't really think it out."
- "The minute I met your mother," my father said, "my **intuition** told me that we'd get married someday."

__ *Intuition* means A. careful study. B. memory. C. instinct.

10 obtrusive
(ŏb-troo͞′sĭv)
-adjective

- The huge, sprawling new mall seemed **obtrusive** in the quiet little country town.
- My brother's stutter is often hardly noticeable, but when he is nervous or in a hurry, it can become **obtrusive**.

__ *Obtrusive* means A. unpleasantly obvious. B. unplanned. C. greatly improved.

Matching Words with Definitions

Following are definitions of the ten words. Clearly write or print each word next to its definition. The sentences above and on the previous page will help you decide on the meaning of each word.

1. ____________________ To treat with scorn or contempt; defy insultingly
2. ____________________ Instinctive knowledge; hunch
3. ____________________ To carry out; put into practice
4. ____________________ Undesirably noticeable
5. ____________________ Wise in keeping silent about secrets and other information of a delicate nature; prudent; tactful
6. ____________________ Performed or spoken without practice or preparation
7. ____________________ Extremely evil; outrageous
8. ____________________ A conclusion drawn from evidence; an assumption
9. ____________________ To add (to something or someone) what is lacking or needed; round out; bring to perfection
10. ____________________ Extremely attentive to details; fussy

CAUTION: Do not go any further until you are sure the above answers are correct. Then you can use the definitions to help you in the following practices. Your goal is eventually to know the words well enough so that you don't need to check the definitions at all.

Sentence Check 1

Using the answer line provided, complete each item below with the correct word from the box. Use each word once.

A. **complement**	B. **discreet**	C. **fastidious**	D. **flout**	E. **heinous**
F. **implement**	G. **impromptu**	H. **inference**	I. **intuition**	J. **obtrusive**

_______________ 1. "Loose lips sink ships" was a famous World War II slogan. It warned Americans to be ___ and not say anything that might reveal military plans.

_______________ 2. The ___ press conference turned out to be a bad idea. The senator should have planned his remarks beforehand.

_______________ 3. In the American system of justice, anyone charged with a crime, no matter how ___ the offense, is entitled to be defended by a lawyer.

_______________ 4. After Rudy ___(e)d his 11 p.m. curfew—breezing in at 2 a.m. with a cheerful "Hi, folks!"—his parents took away his car keys for a month.

_______________ 5. Rachel's ___ told her not to date a man who kept tropical fish in his bathtub.

_______________ 6. When Niko's smartphone lit up in the middle of the dark movie theater, it was so ___ that several people yelled for him to shut it off.

_______________ 7. Alicia signed her card to Manuel "Warm regards." Manuel's ___ was that she meant "I feel *only* warm regards, not love."

_______________ 8. Wendy is an excellent hair stylist, because she doesn't just cut hair. She also advises her customers about which hairstyle will ___ their features.

_______________ 9. The writer Ernest Hemingway had a "tough guy" image but was ___ about using words; he rewrote the ending of one novel forty-four times.

_______________ 10. To ___ their plan for a surprise attack on the girls' club, the boys needed squirt guns and a gallon of grape juice.

NOTE: Now check your answers to these items by turning to page 130. Going over the answers carefully will help you prepare for the next two practices, for which answers are not given.

Sentence Check 2

Using the answer lines provided, complete each item below with **two** words from the box. Use each word once.

____
_______________ 1–2. What Kay actually said was, "It would be ___ not to discuss the missing funds in front of Debra." But she meant us to make this ___: "I think she stole them."

____
_______________ 3–4. The dark, rumbling voice of the bass ___(e)d the high, sweet tones of the soprano as they sang a(n) ___ but flawless duet. Having just met, they were surprised and delighted at how good they sounded together.

____
_______________ 5–6. Although Anne is one of my best friends, my ___ tells me we would not be good roommates. She's so ___ that she irons her bedsheets, while I'm notorious° for giving my apartment sporadic° cleanings—like once a year.

_______________ 7–8. There seems to be a conspiracy° to ___ the rule, "No sidewalk vendors on government property." The vendors have set up their stands in an ___ spot—right in front of City Hall.
____

_______________ 9–10. Connoisseurs° of science fiction love one movie in which evil alien invaders decide to annihilate° all life on Earth. The aliens ___ this ___ plan by constructing a "space shield" that cuts off all sunlight.
____

Final Check: *Harriet Tubman*

Here is a final opportunity for you to strengthen your knowledge of the ten words. First read the following selection carefully. Then fill in each blank with a word from the box at the top of the previous page. (Context clues will help you figure out which word goes in which blank.) Use each word once.

In 1849 Harriet Tubman—then in her late twenties—fled from the (1)_______________ brutality she had endured as a slave. Aware that a lone black woman would be a(n) (2)_______________ figure among ordinary travelers, she traveled on foot and only at night, over hundreds of miles, to reach Pennsylvania. There, for the first time in her life, she was free, but her parents, brothers, and sisters remained behind in Maryland, still slaves. Harriet decided to go back for them—and, over the next ten years, for many more.

© Library of Congress, Prints and Photos Division.

Harriet had several qualities that (3)_______________(e)d each other and facilitated° her mission. First, because she was knowledgeable and had good (4)_______________, she could always sense when an opportune° time for an escape had arrived, and who could and couldn't be trusted. Second, she was (5)_______________ about planning; she always worked out a plan to the last detail before she (6)_______________(e)d it. Third, she was flexible, capable of taking (7)_______________ action if an unexpected problem arose. Time and again, when a disaster seemed unavoidable, she was able to forestall° it. For instance, when she learned that slave-hunters had posted a description of a runaway man, she disguised him as a woman. When the slave-hunters turned up at a railroad station, she fooled them by having the runaways board a southbound train instead of a northbound one. Fourth, she was (8)_______________ about her plans. She knew how important it was to be reticent°, since anyone might be a spy. Often, her instructions about where and when to meet were not actually stated, but were (9)_______________s in the songs and Bible stories she used, familiar to those waiting to escape. Fifth, she was physically strong, able to endure extended periods of deprivation°; she could go for a long time without food, shelter, or rest.

Harriet Tubman (10)_______________(e)d the unjust laws of an evil system, but she was never captured, and she never lost a single runaway. She led more slaves to freedom than any other individual—over three hundred—and her name is venerated° to this day.

Scores Sentence Check 2 _______% Final Check _______%

Enter your scores above and in the **Vocabulary Performance Chart** on the inside back cover of the book.

auspicious	rebuke
expedite	redeem
extenuating	subordinate
fraudulent	transgress
innuendo	vehement

Ten Words in Context

In the space provided, write the letter of the meaning closest to that of each **boldfaced** word. Use the context of the sentences to help you figure out each word's meaning.

1 auspicious
(ô-spĭsh′əs)
-adjective

- The beginning of the semester was **auspicious** for Liza; she got an A on the first quiz and saw this as a promise of more good grades to come.
- Jen and Robert's marriage plans did not get off to an **auspicious** start. They couldn't agree on what kind of ceremony they wanted or which guests to invite.

__ *Auspicious* means A. deceptive. B. indirect. C. favorable.

2 expedite
(ĕks′pə-dīt′)
-verb

- Express lanes in supermarkets **expedite** the checkout process for shoppers who buy only a few items.
- To **expedite** payment on an insurance claim, be sure to include all the necessary information on the form before mailing it in.

__ *Expedite* means A. to hurry up. B. to reduce the cost of. C. to delay.

3 extenuating
(ĕk-stĕn′yo͞o-ā′tĭng)
-adjective

- I know I promised to come to the surprise party, but there were **extenuating** circumstances: my car broke down.
- When my father had a heart attack, I missed a final exam. Due to the **extenuating** circumstances, the professor agreed to let me take a makeup exam.

__ *Extenuating* means A. providing a good excuse. B. assigning blame. C. encouraging.

4 fraudulent
(frô′jə-lənt)
-adjective

- When people make **fraudulent** rather than truthful statements while under oath in court, they could face jail time for breaking the law.
- The art dealer was involved in a **fraudulent** scheme to pass off worthless forgeries as valuable old paintings.

__ *Fraudulent* means A. instructive. B. dishonest. C. careless.

5 innuendo
(ĭn′yo͞o-ĕn′dō)
-noun

- People weren't willing to say directly that the mayor had taken a bribe, but there were many **innuendos** such as "Someone must have gotten to him."
- When Neil said, "Emily's home sick. Again," he was using an **innuendo**. He really meant that she was just taking another day off.

__ *Innuendo* means A. a sharp scolding. B. an obvious lie. C. a suggestion.

6 rebuke
(rĭ-byo͞ok′)
-verb

- When the puppy chews the furniture, don't hit him; instead, **rebuke** him in a harsh voice.
- Although my father scolded me many times in private, I'm grateful that he never **rebuked** me in public.

__ *Rebuke* means A. to criticize. B. to make excuses for. C. to hit.

7 redeem
(rĭ-dēm′)
-verb

- Tuan's parents were angry with him for neglecting his chores, but he **redeemed** himself by washing and waxing their car.
- Cal was suspended from the basketball team because of his low grades, but he **redeemed** himself the next semester by earning a B average.

__ *Redeem* means A. to reveal. B. to make up for past errors. C. to punish.

8 subordinate
(sə-bôr′də-nĭt)
-adjective

- As a waiter, I take orders from the headwaiter, and he's **subordinate** to the manager of the restaurant.
- The federal District Courts are lower than the United States Court of Appeals, which in turn is **subordinate** to the Supreme Court.

__ *Subordinate to* means A. lower than. B. a substitute for. C. superior to.

9 transgress
(trăns-grĕs′)
-verb

- Our dog isn't allowed on the furniture, but he sometimes **transgresses** when he thinks we're not looking.
- Kianna knew she had **transgressed** against family wishes when she sold the ring her grandmother had given her.

__ *Transgress* means A. to benefit. B. to tell a lie. C. to commit an offense.

10 vehement
(vē′ə-mənt)
-adjective

- I knew my parents would not be happy about my plan to take a year off from school, but I didn't expect their objections to be so **vehement**.
- Mrs. Ortiz was **vehement** about her dislike of eBooks. "Give me paper, not a screen!" she proclaimed in class.

__ *Vehement* means A. strong. B. secret. C. relaxed.

Matching Words with Definitions

Following are definitions of the ten words. Clearly write or print each word next to its definition. The sentences above and on the previous page will help you decide on the meaning of each word.

1. ____________________ An indirect remark or gesture, usually suggesting something belittling or improper; an insinuation; a hint
2. ____________________ To speed up or ease the progress of; make easier
3. ____________________ To scold sharply; express blame or disapproval
4. ____________________ Intense; forceful
5. ____________________ Characterized by trickery, cheating, or lies
6. ____________________ Being a good sign; favorable; encouraging
7. ____________________ Serving to make (a fault, an offense, or guilt) less serious or seem less serious through some excuse
8. ____________________ To sin or commit an offense; break a law or command
9. ____________________ Under the authority or power of another; inferior or below another in rank, power, or importance
10. ____________________ To restore (oneself) to favor by making up for offensive conduct; make amends

CAUTION: Do not go any further until you are sure the above answers are correct. Then you can use the definitions to help you in the following practices. Your goal is eventually to know the words well enough so that you don't need to check the definitions at all.

Sentence Check 1

Using the answer line provided, complete each item below with the correct word from the box. Use each word once.

A. **auspicious**	B. **expedite**	C. **extenuating**	D. **fraudulent**	E. **innuendo**
F. **rebuke**	G. **redeem**	H. **subordinate**	I. **transgress**	J. **vehement**

_______ 1. After showing up late for the fundraising dinner and then falling asleep during the speeches, the politician tried to ___ himself with a public apology.

_______ 2. To ___ the registration process, fill out all the forms before you get in line.

_______ 3. If you get a phone call announcing that you've won a free car or free trip in some contest you've never heard of, watch out. It's probably ___.

_______ 4. When young children ___, they may lie to cover up their misdeeds.

_______ 5. The company president is ___ only to the board of directors. She takes orders from the board, and only the board can fire her.

_______ 6. "Yes, my client robbed the bank," the lawyer said, "but there were ___ circumstances. She didn't have time to wait in line to make a withdrawal."

_______ 7. The friendly weekly poker game grew less friendly when Travis said, "Isn't it amazing that, week after week, Bill always wins?" The ___, of course, was that Bill was cheating.

_______ 8. Edna was ___ in her opposition to the proposed budget cuts. She let everyone in the department know just how strongly she felt.

_______ 9. Later, Edna's supervisor ___(e)d her, saying, "No one asked for your opinion about the budget, so just get on with your work."

_______ 10. According to tradition, it's ___ if March "comes in like a lion" with stormy weather, because it will then "go out like a lamb."

NOTE: Now check your answers to these items by turning to page 130. Going over the answers carefully will help you prepare for the next two practices, for which answers are not given.

Sentence Check 2

Using the answer lines provided, complete each item below with **two** words from the box. Use each word once.

____
_______ 1–2. The tour did not get off to a(n) ___ start—the singer missed the first concert. But there was a(n) ___ reason: he had developed bronchitis, and trying to sing would have exacerbated° the infection.

____
_______ 3–4. First the judge ___(e)d the fake "doctor" for "violating the public trust." Then he fined him thousands of dollars for engaging in ___ advertising.

____
_______ 5–6. Reuben certainly ___(e)d against decorum° when he showed up at his sister's wedding in jeans. Later, he tried to ___ himself by giving the newlyweds an ostentatious° present.

____
____

7–8. The restaurant critic wrote, "Those customers who are oblivious° to the headwaiter's outstretched hand will have an overly long wait to be seated." Her ___ implied that customers could ___ getting a table only by slipping the headwaiter some money.

____
____

9–10. The owner of that company is ___ in his insistence that managers implement° a plan to communicate better with workers in ___ positions.

Final Check: *Tony's Rehabilitation*

Here is a final opportunity for you to strengthen your knowledge of the ten words. First read the following selection carefully. Then fill in each blank with a word from the box at the top of the previous page. (Context clues will help you figure out which word goes in which blank.) Use each word once.

When he was 18, Tony was arrested for possessing a small amount of cocaine. Instead of panicking, he was nonchalant°. He didn't think of himself as having (1)_______________(e)d; the cocaine was just for fun, not some heinous° offense. On the way to the police station, he wasn't worried about being interrogated°. He figured he could claim that there were (2)_______________ circumstances. He'd say he was just holding the stuff for a friend—maybe he'd even insinuate° that the "friend" was making him the victim of some (3)_______________ scheme—and then he'd be released right away.

But things didn't work out according to Tony's plan. When he told his story to the police captain, the captain's response was hardly (4)_______________: "Tell it to the judge, kid. I've heard it all before." Then, turning to a(n) (5)_______________ officer, the captain said, "Book him." Tony still wasn't distraught°. He just thought, "Well, my father will extricate° me from this mess. He'll (6)_______________ me, of course, but after he's through yelling at me, he'll pay my bail, even if it's exorbitant°. And he knows plenty of influential people who can (7)_______________ the legal process so my case will be dismissed quickly." So Tony wasn't prepared for his father's (8)_______________ anger, or for his parting words: "You got yourself into this. Now you'll take the consequences."

With no bail, Tony had to remain in jail until his hearing took place. He was terrified, especially by the other inmates. Some were trying to start fights; others used (9)_______________s, such as calling him "the millionaire." His inference° was that they were threatening retribution° for his easy life. He got through his nine-day stay without being attacked, though, and the experience woke up his good sense. He realized that fooling around with drugs is insidious°—his involvement would only get worse unless he turned his life around.

Therefore, at his court hearing, Tony asked to be sent to a drug treatment center, and as a first-time offender, he got his wish. Today, six years later, Tony is still "clean." He has not regressed° to his previous self-destructive behavior. And he still wonders what would have become of him if he hadn't managed to (10)_______________ himself.

Scores Sentence Check 2 ________% Final Check ________%

Enter your scores above and in the **Vocabulary Performance Chart** on the inside back cover of the book.

CHAPTER 19

deride	misconstrue
derogatory	paramount
fabricate	quandary
impending	turbulent
macabre	validate

Ten Words in Context

In the space provided, write the letter of the meaning closest to that of each **boldfaced** word. Use the context of the sentences to help you figure out each word's meaning.

1 deride
(dĭ-rīd′)
-verb

- One nightclub comedian **derides** members of the audience, poking fun at their looks, clothing, and mannerisms. He says they know it's just part of the act.
- Walter went on a diet after several classmates **derided** him by calling him "Lardo" and "Blimpy."

__ *Deride* means A. to misunderstand. B. to mock. C. to argue with.

2 derogatory
(dĭ-rŏg′ə-tôr′ē)
-adjective

- Lorenzo's **derogatory** remark about his boss—he called her an airhead—caused him to get fired.
- Charisse makes **derogatory** comments about Deion behind his back, saying that he's vain, sloppy, and lazy. But she never says such things to his face.

__ *Derogatory* means A. uncomplimentary. B. mistaken. C. provable.

3 fabricate
(făb′rĭ-kāt′)
-verb

- Supermarket tabloids often **fabricate** ridiculous stories, such as "Boy Is Born Wearing Green Sneakers."
- After she was caught scribbling on the wall, the little girl **fabricated** this excuse: "A clown came into my room and did it."

__ *Fabricate* means A. to avoid. B. to prove. C. to invent.

4 impending
(ĭm-pĕnd′ĭng)
-adjective

- Gary never studies until an exam is **impending**. If he'd start sooner, he wouldn't have to cram so hard, and he'd get better grades.
- "Because of the company's **impending** move," the office manager said, "I'm not ordering any supplies until next month, when we'll be in the new office."

__ *Impending* means A. approaching. B. apparent. C. important.

5 macabre
(mə-kŏb′rə)
-adjective

- Edgar Allan Poe's story "The Fall of the House of Usher" is a **macabre** tale in which someone is buried alive.
- The movie opened with a **macabre** scene: a row of bodies lying in drawers in the city morgue.

__ *Macabre* means A. confusing. B. mocking. C. gruesome.

6 misconstrue
(mĭs′kən-stro͞o′)
-verb

- Carla would like to date Matt, but when she told him she was busy last weekend, he **misconstrued** her meaning, thinking she wasn't interested in him.
- Many readers **misconstrue** Robert Frost's well-known line "Good fences make good neighbors." They think it's Frost's own opinion, but the line is spoken by an unneighborly character.

__ *Misconstrue* means A. to misunderstand. B. to understand. C. to ignore.

7 paramount
(păr′ə-mount′)
-adjective

- When you are driving on rain-slick, icy, or winding roads, good traction is of **paramount** importance, so always be sure your tires are in top condition.
- **Paramount** Pictures must have chosen its name to suggest that its movies were superior to all others.

__ *Paramount* means A. supreme. B. growing. C. successful.

8 quandary
(kwŏn′də-rē)
-noun

- Bonita was in a **quandary**—she couldn't decide whether to return to school, take a job she had just been offered, or move to Alaska with her family.
- Aaron is in a **quandary** over financial matters: he is baffled by the problems of making a budget, handling credit, and paying taxes.

__ *Quandary* means A. a state of confusion. B. a state of anger. C. a state of confidence.

9 turbulent
(tûr′byo͞o-lənt)
-adjective

- The **turbulent** air made the plane rock so wildly that passengers felt as if they were on a roller coaster.
- The Warreners' household tends to be **turbulent**. Whenever Mr. Warrener gets upset, he yells and throws things.

__ *Turbulent* means A. violent. B. distant. C. unusual.

10 validate
(văl′ə-dāt′)
-verb

- Many people believe Columbus sailed west to **validate** the theory that the world is round. But in 1492, the fact that the world is round was already well known.
- There is no real doubt about the dangers of smoking; the claim that smoking is a serious health risk has been **validated** by many studies.

__ *Validate* means A. to misinterpret. B. to prove. C. to invent.

Matching Words with Definitions

Following are definitions of the ten words. Clearly write or print each word next to its definition. The sentences above and on the previous page will help you decide on the meaning of each word.

1. ______________ Full of wild disorder or wildly irregular motion; violently disturbed
2. ______________ Suggestive of death and decay; frightful; causing horror and disgust
3. ______________ A state of uncertainty or confusion about what to do; predicament
4. ______________ Expressing a low opinion; belittling
5. ______________ To show to be true; prove; confirm
6. ______________ To misinterpret; misunderstand the meaning or significance of
7. ______________ To make fun of; ridicule
8. ______________ To make up (a story, information) in order to deceive; invent (a lie)
9. ______________ About to happen; imminent
10. ______________ Of greatest concern or importance; foremost; chief in rank or authority

CAUTION: Do not go any further until you are sure the above answers are correct. Then you can use the definitions to help you in the following practices. Your goal is eventually to know the words well enough so that you don't need to check the definitions at all.

Sentence Check 1

Using the answer line provided, complete each item below with the correct word from the box. Use each word once.

A. **deride**	B. **derogatory**	C. **fabricate**	D. **impending**	E. **macabre**
F. **misconstrue**	G. **paramount**	H. **quandary**	I. **turbulent**	J. **validate**

________ 1. When my friend said her teacher was "different," I wasn't sure if she meant the description to be complimentary or ___.

________ 2. Delia ___(e)d Miguel's friendliness as romantic interest. She didn't realize that he already had a girlfriend.

________ 3. Just before I was fired, I had a sense of ___ disaster; I could tell that something bad was about to happen.

________ 4. We had skipped dinner in order to get to the play on time, so throughout the performance, food—not the drama—was ___ in our thoughts.

________ 5. Mel has a(n) ___ hobby—he visits places where murders were committed.

________ 6. A critic once ___(e)d a book he disliked by saying, "This is not a novel to be tossed aside lightly. It should be thrown with great force."

________ 7. The sun may seem to be shining calmly and steadily, but in fact, nuclear reactions inside the sun are causing a seething mass of ___ flames.

________ 8. Ivan is in a ___ over his car. He doesn't know whether to get his old car the major repairs it desperately needs, take out a loan and buy his dream car, or spend the money he has on another used car he doesn't like.

________ 9. In the psychology class, the students were given an interesting team assignment. They had to make some statement about human nature and then ___ it by finding supporting evidence.

________ 10. Dwayne didn't show up for the final exam because he hadn't studied, but he ___(e)d a story about having a flat tire.

NOTE: Now check your answers to these items by turning to page 130. Going over the answers carefully will help you prepare for the next two practices, for which answers are not given.

Sentence Check 2

Using the answer lines provided, complete each item below with **two** words from the box. Use each word once.

____
________ 1–2. I was in a ___ over whether to study, practice the piano, or go to a movie with my friend Sal. To complicate things further, Sal wanted to see a(n) ___ horror film, and I dislike anything gruesome.

____
________ 3–4. Many surfers prefer ___ water to calmer waves. Their ___ goal is excitement, and they get a feeling of exhilaration° from confronting a dangerous situation.

______________ ______________ 5–6. When Craig called Peggy "the perfect secretary," she was offended. He was complimenting her, but she ___(e)d his comment, thinking he had ___(e)d her by saying she belonged in a lesser position.

______________ ______________ 7–8. With the trial ___, the defense lawyer tried to forestall° negative news stories by asking for a "gag" order. The lawyer argued that if ___ stories about his client's character were published, the trial would be a travesty° of justice.

______________ ______________ 9–10. When the evidence does not ___ their theories, scrupulous° researchers will report this honestly. But less conscientious researchers will flout° scientific ethics and ___ fake "results" to appear to prove their theories.

Final Check: *Rumors*

Here is a final opportunity for you to strengthen your knowledge of the ten words. First read the following selection carefully. Then fill in each blank with a word from the box at the top of the previous page. (Context clues will help you figure out which word goes in which blank.) Use each word once.

Did you hear that K-Mart sold sweaters with baby snakes inside? The story, of course, was untrue, but it was not easy to squelch°.

How do such unrealistic rumors get started? Sometimes they are (1)______________(e)d. In the case of the K-Mart rumor, the story was actually fraudulent°; someone had deliberately made it up and spread it to discredit the store. Often, though, a rumor starts with an innocent misinterpretation. For instance, when a magazine article drew an analogy° between a worm farm turning out bait and McDonald's turning out hamburgers, some readers (2)______________(e)d this to mean that McDonald's was grinding up worms in its burgers—and the ridiculous story spread.

© Todd Taulman Photography/shutterstock.com

Rumors about individuals can start when someone makes a(n) (3)______________ statement or (4)______________s someone else, out of rancor° or jealousy: "Josie got an A because the professor is friends with her parents," or "Al isn't in class today—he left town because he knew his arrest for stealing a copy of the final exam was (5)______________." Even an innuendo°—something that's merely hinted at—can start a rumor that can do permanent harm to someone's reputation: "Isn't Josie lucky that her parents are such good friends with the professor?" No story is too gruesome to make the rounds, not even the (6)______________ tale of the girl whose beehive hairdo housed a black widow spider, which eventually burrowed into her brain and killed her.

Once a rumor gets started, people who hear it are sometimes in a (7)______________. Even if there's nothing to support the rumor, they may be afraid to ignore it. And so there is an explosion of rumors, spreading fear, damaging reputations, and turning calm situations into (8)______________ ones. To stop or forestall° rumors, one thing is probably of (9)______________ importance: before accepting any story, be sure the facts (10)______________ it.

Scores Sentence Check 2 ________% Final Check ________%

Enter your scores above and in the **Vocabulary Performance Chart** on the inside back cover of the book.

abrasive	emulate
admonish	hierarchy
antithesis	incapacitate
culmination	prognosis
docile	tumult

Ten Words in Context

In the space provided, write the letter of the meaning closest to that of each **boldfaced** word. Use the context of the sentences to help you figure out each word's meaning.

1 abrasive
(ə-brā′sĭv)
-adjective

- Pumice stone, a naturally **abrasive** substance, can be used for rubbing away rough spots on the feet.
- Roz has an **abrasive** personality—critical and negative. She always seems to rub people the wrong way.

___ *Abrasive* means A. simple. B. harsh. C. common.

2 admonish
(ăd-mŏn′ĭsh)
-verb

- When the guide found the hikers deep in the woods but unhurt, he **admonished** them for straying off the trail.
- Because the little girl had spent her entire allowance on candy, her parents **admonished** her for wasting her money.

___ *Admonish* means A. to lead. B. to criticize. C. to irritate.

3 antithesis
(ăn-tĭth′ĭ-sĭs)
-noun

- My taste in music is the **antithesis** of my brother's. I like heavy metal, played loud; he likes soft classical music.
- Pauline's free-spirited second husband is the **antithesis** of her first, who was a very timid and cautious man.

___ *Antithesis* means A. the reverse. B. something superior. C. an imitation.

4 culmination
(kŭl′mə-nā′shən)
-noun

- For an actor or actress, receiving an Academy Award is often the **culmination** of many years of effort, progressing from drama school to bit parts to major roles.
- The Super Bowl is the **culmination** of the entire professional football season. All the rivalries, victories, and defeats lead up to this final contest.

___ *Culmination* means A. a series. B. a cause. C. a final high point.

5 docile
(dŏs′ĭl)
-adjective

- After only a month of obedience training, our uncontrollable puppy calmed down, learned to pay attention to us, and became far more **docile**.
- Drugs and even surgery have been used in mental hospitals to make violent patients **docile**, so that they could be managed more easily.

___ *Docile* means A. obedient. B. strong. C. curable.

6 emulate
(ĕm′yo͞o-lāt′)
-verb

- Jessie has always tried to **emulate** her older sister; she tries hard to do just as well as her sister—if not better—in school, at sports, and in popularity.
- Youngsters often want to **emulate** famous athletes. They train almost as hard as the champions do, with dreams of someday being as skilled as their heroes.

___ *Emulate* means A. to admire. B. to imitate. C. to submit to.

7 hierarchy
(hī′ər-âr′kē)
-noun

- The armed forces are a clear example of a strict **hierarchy**. Everyone has a specific rank and must follow the orders of those whose rank is higher.
- Eva soon learned that all requests and suggestions had to be passed up through the levels of the company **hierarchy**. She could communicate directly with her own boss, but not with the boss's boss—let alone with the company president.

__ *Hierarchy* means A. a ranked system. B. a training system. C. a large system.

8 incapacitate
(ĭn′kə-păs′ə-tāt′)
-verb

- The lecture was canceled because the speaker was **incapacitated** by the flu.
- Terrence's extreme fear of public speaking **incapacitated** him last night. When called on to make a speech at the awards banquet, he stared silently out at the audience.

__ *Incapacitate* means A. to irritate. B. to be concerned with. C. to disable.

9 prognosis
(prŏg-nō′sĭs)
-noun

- Nathan's operation went well. The surgeon's **prognosis** is that Nathan will fully recover.
- Unless something can be done to reduce global warming, the **prognosis** for the environment will remain poor.

__ *Prognosis* means A. a forecast. B. an illness. C. an organization.

10 tumult
(to͞o′mŭlt′)
-noun

- Spectators at a hockey match are often wild and noisy, and the **tumult** becomes even greater during a "sudden-death" overtime.
- On New Year's Eve, the **tumult** in Times Square reaches such proportions that the crowd noise can be heard a mile away.

__ *Tumult* means A. damage. B. uproar. C. friction.

Matching Words with Definitions

Following are definitions of the ten words. Clearly write or print each word next to its definition. The sentences above and on the previous page will help you decide on the meaning of each word.

1. ________________ The noisy disorder of a crowd; a commotion
2. ________________ To make unable or unfit, especially for normal activities; disable
3. ________________ Tending to give in to the control or power of others without resisting; easy to handle or discipline; willingly led
4. ________________ Able to cause a wearing away by rubbing or scraping; rough; irritating
5. ________________ A prediction of the course, outcome, or fate of something, especially a disease or injury
6. ________________ To scold gently but seriously; caution; give a warning
7. ________________ The exact opposite
8. ________________ The highest point or degree of a series of actions or events; the climax
9. ________________ To try to equal or surpass, especially by imitation; imitate
10. ________________ An organization of people in a series of levels, according to importance or authority

CAUTION: Do not go any further until you are sure the above answers are correct. Then you can use the definitions to help you in the following practices. Your goal is eventually to know the words well enough so that you don't need to check the definitions at all.

Sentence Check 1

Using the answer line provided, complete each item below with the correct word from the box. Use each word once.

A. abrasive	B. admonish	C. antithesis	D. culmination	E. docile
F. emulate	G. hierarchy	H. incapacitate	I. prognosis	J. tumult

______ 1. The ___ of the Roman Catholic Church goes from the parish priest up through bishops, archbishops, and cardinals, to the Pope at the head.

______ 2. Wendell's ideas about furniture are the ___ of mine. He likes colonial maple, but I like ultramodern tubular steel.

______ 3. The runner was ___(e)d by a sprained ankle and had to miss the big race.

______ 4. I ruined a nonstick frying pan by using a(n) ___ cleanser on it—the surface rubbed right off.

______ 5. At the rock concert, the audience grew more and more excited and out of control. There was such ___ that no one could hear the music.

______ 6. Young people often try to ___ celebrities, imitating their clothing, hairstyles, and manner of speaking.

______ 7. In colonial America, many people believed in and feared witches. Hysteria over "witch-hunting" reached its ___ in Salem, Massachusetts, where nineteen supposed witches were put to death.

______ 8. In the prison movie, the convicts acted very ___ while planning a riot. The guards—who weren't too bright—kept congratulating the inmates on being so well-behaved.

______ 9. The company is financially sick, and unless some changes are made in top management, the ___ is poor—it could go out of business.

______ 10. Mother ___(e)d us for spending too much money on her birthday gift, but we could see that she was pleased.

NOTE: Now check your answers to these items by turning to page 130. Going over the answers carefully will help you prepare for the next two practices, for which answers are not given.

Sentence Check 2

Using the answer lines provided, complete each item below with **two** words from the box. Use each word once.

______
______ 1–2. The ___ for Dale's arthritis is not encouraging. Her doctor didn't equivocate° but told her frankly that in time it might ___ her completely.

______
______ 3–4. The rebellious little girl, always demanding more and more independence, was the ___ of her obedient, ___ sister. They were an incongruous° pair of siblings.

_______________ _______________ 5–6. Gil didn't expect the children's behavior in the car to be impeccable°, but the ___ in the back seat finally reached such a level that he had to ___ them.

_______________ _______________ 7–8. Cory has many good qualities that I would like to ___. But his ___ manner is a handicap; he estranges° people because he rejects any ideas that differ from his own.

_______________ _______________ 9–10. Beth moved steadily up the company ___ until she was named president. This appointment, the ___ of twenty years of hard work and dedication, put her at the zenith° of her career.

Final Check: *Firing Our Boss*

Here is a final opportunity for you to strengthen your knowledge of the ten words. First read the following selection carefully. Then fill in each blank with a word from the box at the top of the previous page. (Context clues will help you figure out which word goes in which blank.) Use each word once.

My stint° in the bookkeeping department had lasted for three years when Jay Keller was brought in as department head. I don't expect supervisors to be pals with their staff, and I don't object to being (1)_______________(e)d when I've done something wrong. Keller's criticism, however, was constant and harsh, and the office atmosphere seemed permeated° by his contempt toward us. His (2)_______________ style made everyone in the department miserable. Keller was the complete (3)_______________ of Chandra Borden, our previous boss, who had been so thoughtful and solicitous° about our needs that we all tried to (4)_______________ her. In contrast, Keller's mere presence could (5)_______________ us to a point where we could hardly add two and two.

© Thomas McFarlan/123rf.com

Within a few weeks, even the most (6)_______________ employees were becoming rebellious and starting to have subversive° thoughts. Our frustration and anger finally reached its (7)_______________ when Keller loudly belittled a new worker in front of everyone else, using such derogatory° terms ("Stupid! Airhead!") that he made her cry. Furious, we suddenly decided that our only option was to go over Keller's head—to ignore the company (8)_______________ and, as a group, present our vehement° complaint about Keller directly to his boss.

Our meeting in her office began in (9)_______________, but then we settled down and told our story, trying to be as lucid° as possible so she could understand exactly what had been going on. We concluded with the argument that ours was a deeply troubled department and that if Keller stayed, the (10)_______________ for it was not good: everyone else would quit. That was Friday afternoon. On Monday morning, our group effort proved to be successful: we had a new boss.

Scores Sentence Check 2 ________% Final Check ________%

Enter your scores above and in the **Vocabulary Performance Chart** on the inside back cover of the book.

UNIT FOUR: Review

The box at the right lists twenty-five words from Unit Four. Using the clues at the bottom of the page, fill in these words to complete the puzzle that follows.

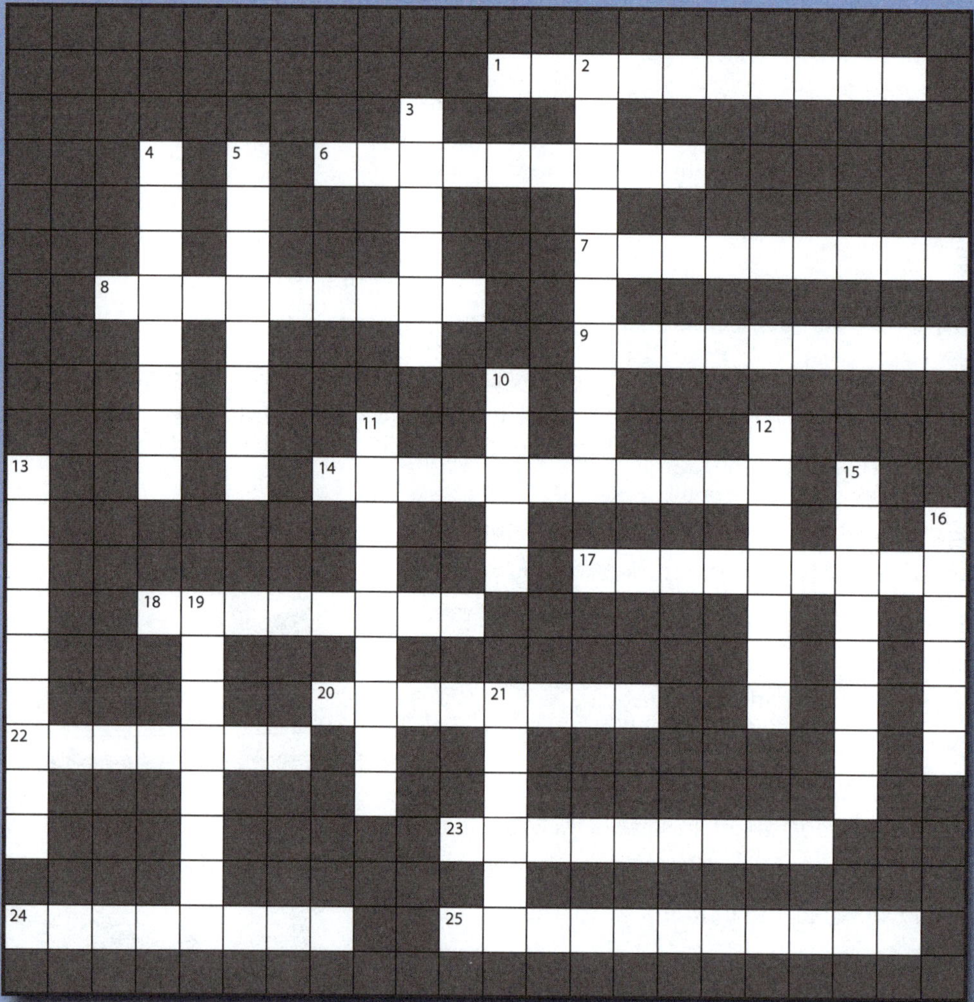

abrasive
admonish
auspicious
discreet
disparity
docile
emulate
expedite
flout
forestall
fraudulent
heinous
impending
implement
insinuate
intuition
misconstrue
permeate
prognosis
quandary
rebuke
redeem
retribution
turbulent
validate

ACROSS

1. Characterized by trickery, cheating, or lies
6. A prediction of the course or outcome of something
7. About to happen; imminent
8. To prevent or hinder by taking action beforehand
9. The ability to know something without reasoning
14. To misinterpret
17. To suggest slyly
18. To show to be true; prove
20. Wise in keeping silent about secrets; prudent; tactful
22. To try to equal or surpass, especially by imitation
23. Full of wild disorder; violently disturbed
24. To flow or spread throughout (something)
25. Something given or done as repayment, reward, or (usually) punishment

DOWN

2. Being a good sign; favorable; encouraging
3. Tending to give in to the control or power of others without resisting; willingly led
4. To scold gently but seriously
5. To speed up or ease the progress of
10. To treat with scorn or contempt
11. An inequality or difference, as in ages or amounts
12. Extremely evil; outrageous
13. To carry out; put into practice
15. A state of uncertainty or confusion about what to do
16. To restore (oneself) to favor by making up for offensive conduct; make amends
19. Able to cause a wearing away by rubbing or scraping; rough; irritating
21. To scold sharply; express blame or disapproval

UNIT FOUR: Test 1

PART A

Choose the word that best completes each item and write it in the space provided.

_______________ 1. Since petting an animal appears to lower a person's blood pressure, the ___ for survival after a heart attack is probably better for people with pets.

A. prognosis B. culmination C. innuendo D. quandary

_______________ 2. Victor and Raquel ___ each other nicely as business partners. He's detail-oriented but poor at communication; she's disorganized but excellent at public relations.

A. complement B. fabricate C. implement D. validate

_______________ 3. Since my uncle was made vice president of his company, he's ___ only to the president.

A. subordinate B. abrasive C. vehement D. omnipotent

_______________ 4. The mayor ___ citizens for their lack of cooperation in keeping the parks and streets clean.

A. emulated B. rebuked C. fabricated D. validated

_______________ 5. Harsh rules ___ life in Puritan New England, where people were forbidden even to celebrate Christmas.

A. emulated B. permeated C. derided D. redeemed

_______________ 6. For days, Heather planned how she would introduce herself to Ryan, but she never had the courage to ___ her plan.

A. transgress B. complement C. implement D. admonish

_______________ 7. Since I needed the scholarship form as soon as possible, I downloaded it from the college's website to ___ receiving it.

A. insinuate B. forestall C. expedite D. deride

_______________ 8. A novelist once commented on how wonderfully ___ a writer feels when creating "an entire universe."

A. derogatory B. omnipotent C. extenuating D. insidious

_______________ 9. When my foot falls asleep, it ___ me for several minutes.

A. interrogates B. incapacitates C. validates D. insinuates

_______________ 10. The man's ___ maltreatment of his horses left them crippled and starving.

A. docile B. obsequious C. heinous D. paramount

(Continues on next page)

PART B

On the answer line, write the letter of the choice that best completes each item.

____ 11. Brendan has forgotten his girlfriend's birthday. If he **fabricates** an excuse, he might tell her,
- A. "I forgot. I'm sorry. Can I make it up to you tomorrow?"
- B. "I put the money for your gift in my wallet, and someone stole it."
- C. "Birthdays! Who can remember them? They come along so often!"
- D. "If it will make you feel better, you can forget my birthday next June."

____ 12. My brother embarrassed me in front of my date by telling the story of the time I made dinner and the whole family got food poisoning. Later, he **redeemed** himself by
- A. telling another story about me that made me seem brave, funny, and intelligent.
- B. telling even more embarrassing stories about me.
- C. getting into a fight with my date.
- D. asking my date, "Why in the world do you want to go out with her?"

____ 13. People generally use an **innuendo** when they want to say
- A. something critical, but in an indirect way.
- B. something highly complimentary.
- C. something that is not true.
- D. something in praise of themselves.

____ 14. Because Katya felt that her foreign accent was **obtrusive**, she decided to
- A. take a speech class to make it less obvious.
- B. keep it because she liked the way it sounded.
- C. assume that no one would notice it.
- D. emphasize it.

____ 15. Delia knew she must have **transgressed** somehow while driving to work because
- A. she got to work half an hour early.
- B. she found herself in a strange neighborhood.
- C. a police car was following her.
- D. she got to work half an hour late.

____ 16. To **forestall** seeing Diana at school today, Marc
- A. said nasty things to her in the hallway right before classes started.
- B. stayed home.
- C. asked her to eat lunch with him.
- D. ignored her in math class, even though she waved at him.

____ 17. One group of students **flouted** the library's "no unnecessary noise" rule by
- A. complaining about other students who were talking loudly.
- B. making occasional, brief whispered comments to one another.
- C. deliberately dropping heavy books on the floor and then laughing.
- D. studying in absolute silence.

____ 18. When Tara came to work late for the third time that week, her boss's **vehement** response was
- A. "Honey, are you having some sort of problem at home?"
- B. "Good morning, Tara."
- C. "Get out of here and stay out!"
- D. to shake her head and look disappointed.

____ 19. You would be most likely to expect a **tumult** in the midst of a(n)
- A. riot.
- B. church service.
- C. living room where a family was reading.
- D. art museum.

____ 20. Although the prisoner appeared at first to be **docile**, prison officials soon learned he was actually
- A. laid-back, relaxed, and cooperative.
- B. highly intelligent.
- C. depressed to the point of suicide.
- D. rebellious and impossible to discipline.

Score (Number correct) ________ x 5 = ________%

Enter your score above and in the **Vocabulary Performance Chart** on the inside back cover of the book.

UNIT FOUR: Test 2

PART A

Complete each item with a word from the box. Use each word once.

A. **abrasive**	B. **antithesis**	C. **emulate**	D. **extenuating**	E. **fraudulent**
F. **hierarchy**	G. **impromptu**	H. **inference**	I. **interrogate**	J. **intuition**
K. **misconstrue**	L. **quandary**	M. **validate**		

________________ 1. Acting students often perform ___ scenes. Without a script, they must fully imagine how a particular character might speak and behave.

________________ 2. The study ___(e)d claims that drinking is strongly related to violence, providing evidence that alcohol is involved in almost half of all murders in the United States.

________________ 3. Last year, the town experienced a sizzling summer that was the ___ of its frigid winters.

________________ 4. My ___ told me to stay away from anyone who called me "darling" after only five minutes of acquaintance.

________________ 5. I tried to ___ my sister's ability to make money, but I ended up imitating only her readiness to spend it.

________________ 6. The defending lawyer ___(e)d the witness, asking questions about the witness's relationship to the woman who had been murdered.

________________ 7. City streets with names like Oak, Pine, and Elm seem ___ when there aren't any trees on the streets.

________________ 8. Suki is in a(n) ___ as to whether she should start college now part-time or wait until she can go full-time.

________________ 9. The police officer didn't consider my being late for a party a(n) ___ circumstance, so he went ahead and wrote the ticket for speeding.

________________ 10. In Andrea's ___ of values, looks are at the top and honesty is at the bottom.

________________ 11. "Paris" is the name of a new clothing store, but many people ___ it, thinking it's the name of a French restaurant.

________________ 12. Don't use a(n) ___ cleanser on your car. It will rub the paint off.

________________ 13. When Hal refused to kiss his wife goodbye, her ___ was that he was still angry with her.

(Continues on next page)

PART B

Write **C** if the italicized word is used **correctly**. Write **I** if the word is used **incorrectly**.

____ 14. Because my friend phoned at an *opportune* time—just before the end of a suspenseful mystery—I hurriedly asked, "Can I call you back?"

____ 15. My grandmother was always *fastidious* about her long hair. Now that she's unable to care for herself, we make sure that her hair is as clean and perfectly braided as always.

____ 16. As *obsequious* as ever, Daniel refused to get in line for the fire drill.

____ 17. The book's number-one place on the best-seller list was the *culmination* of months of advertising efforts.

____ 18. Just as humans often *admonish* each other by shaking hands, elephants often greet each other by intertwining their trunks.

____ 19. Bonnie is so *discreet* that the minute someone tells her a secret, she gets on the phone to pass it along.

____ 20. It would be fitting *retribution* if my brother, who stares at his smartphone screen for hours at a time, had to live in a region with no internet service.

____ 21. Margery's remark about Jeff's new beard was certainly *derogatory*. She said to him, "You look like an armpit."

____ 22. We had a *turbulent* day at the park, just relaxing on the grass, snoozing, and enjoying the picnic we had packed.

____ 23. There's a large *disparity* in ages between Arlene's two daughters. The elder one is more like a mother to the younger one than a sister.

____ 24. Lightning and thunder are signs of an *impending* storm.

____ 25. The circus clown's beaming smile and *insidious* makeup made all the children at the party laugh.

Score (Number correct) ________ x 4 = ________%

Enter your score above and in the **Vocabulary Performance Chart** on the inside back cover of the book.

UNIT FOUR: Test 3

PART A: Synonyms

In the space provided, write the letter of the choice that is most nearly the **same** in meaning as the **boldfaced** word.

____ 1. **culmination** A. high point B. operation C. revenge D. inspiration

____ 2. **hierarchy** A. ranked arrangement B. imaginary illness C. forecast D. end product

____ 3. **prognosis** A. prevention B. guess C. looking back D. prediction

____ 4. **fabricate** A. admit B. lie C. joke D. err

____ 5. **intuition** A. talent B. instinct C. skill D. memory

____ 6. **emulate** A. imitate B. admire C. praise D. agree with

____ 7. **impending** A. punishing B. unplanned C. suggested D. coming

____ 8. **admonish** A. avoid B. distract C. scold D. dislike

____ 9. **opportune** A. early B. intense C. easy to handle D. well-timed

____ 10. **abrasive** A. unsociable B. unskilled C. violent D. rough

____ 11. **extenuating** A. pleasing B. excusing C. delaying D. creating

____ 12. **incapacitate** A. strengthen B. discourage C. disable D. blame

____ 13. **discreet** A. odd B. well-planned C. favorable D. tactful

____ 14. **implement** A. plan B. carry out C. complete D. delay

____ 15. **quandary** A. dilemma B. solution C. sin D. punishment

____ 16. **disparity** A. inequality B. tact C. too little D. addition

____ 17. **validate** A. question B. study C. prove D. doubt

____ 18. **retribution** A. crime B. repayment C. confession D. innocence

____ 19. **inference** A. denial B. question C. assumption D. omission

____ 20. **vehement** A. tame B. wild C. weak D. forceful

____ 21. **permeate** A. attack B. penetrate C. ease D. hold off

____ 22. **innuendo** A. indirect remark B. question C. opposite D. impression

____ 23. **misconstrue** A. mistrust B. misplace C. mislead D. misunderstand

____ 24. **redeem** A. sin B. leave C. ask D. make up for misbehavior

____ 25. **insinuate** A. suggest B. disagree C. agree D. scold

(Continues on next page)

PART B: Antonyms

In the space provided, write the letter of the choice that is most nearly the **opposite** in meaning to the **boldfaced** word.

		A	B	C	D
____	26. **deride**	A. praise	B. suggest	C. explain	D. annoy
____	27. **insidious**	A. inconvenient	B. strong	C. expert	D. harmless
____	28. **omnipotent**	A. powerless	B. unwilling	C. unknown	D. last
____	29. **antithesis**	A. opposite	B. same	C. compliment	D. insult
____	30. **derogatory**	A. quiet	B. correct	C. smooth	D. flattering
____	31. **paramount**	A. weak	B. unsuccessful	C. unimportant	D. unknown
____	32. **fastidious**	A. neglectful	B. ignorant	C. far	D. slow
____	33. **transgress**	A. change	B. accomplish	C. deny	D. obey
____	34. **forestall**	A. prevent	B. encourage	C. enter	D. leave
____	35. **complement**	A. substitute	B. imitate	C. clash	D. blame
____	36. **docile**	A. clever	B. ungrateful	C. young	D. wild
____	37. **subordinate**	A. alike	B. different	C. inferior	D. superior
____	38. **auspicious**	A. unfavorable	B. unsatisfied	C. private	D. stated directly
____	39. **tumult**	A. loneliness	B. peace and quiet	C. aid	D. slow
____	40. **impromptu**	A. implied	B. performed	C. skillful	D. planned
____	41. **obsequious**	A. playful	B. tired	C. bossy	D. local
____	42. **interrogate**	A. notice	B. answer	C. wonder	D. leave
____	43. **heinous**	A. educated	B. talented	C. good	D. reliable
____	44. **turbulent**	A. calm	B. interesting	C. faithful	D. clear
____	45. **macabre**	A. realistic	B. educational	C. truthful	D. delightful
____	46. **flout**	A. catch	B. respect	C. disprove	D. state directly
____	47. **obtrusive**	A. inconspicuous	B. polite	C. up-to-date	D. clever
____	48. **expedite**	A. remain	B. include	C. delay	D. cover up
____	49. **rebuke**	A. review	B. consider	C. judge	D. praise
____	50. **fraudulent**	A. helpful	B. honest	C. friendly	D. hard-working

Score (Number correct) ________ x 2 = ________%

Enter your score above and in the **Vocabulary Performance Chart** on the inside back cover of the book.

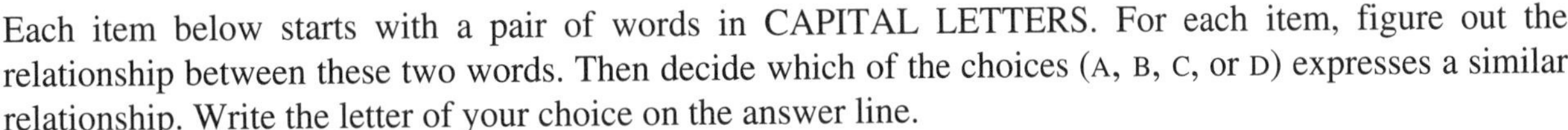

UNIT FOUR: Test 4

Each item below starts with a pair of words in CAPITAL LETTERS. For each item, figure out the relationship between these two words. Then decide which of the choices (A, B, C, or D) expresses a similar relationship. Write the letter of your choice on the answer line.

____ 1. FRAUDULENT : HONEST ::
- A. foolhardy : senseless
- B. freakish : odd
- C. stale : fresh
- D. fruitful : productive

____ 2. SUBORDINATE : ASSISTANT ::
- A. superior : boss
- B. persistent : architect
- C. humorous : librarian
- D. noble : beggar

____ 3. OMNIPOTENT : HELPLESS ::
- A. sensible : unreasonable
- B. kind : helpful
- C. mighty : powerful
- D. recent : new

____ 4. OPPORTUNE : WELL-TIMED ::
- A. working : broken
- B. delayed : ahead of time
- C. punctual : on time
- D. frequent : rare

____ 5. DISCREET : DIPLOMAT ::
- A. hasty : tightrope walker
- B. frail : piano mover
- C. shy : master of ceremonies
- D. interesting : speaker

____ 6. FASTIDIOUS : NEGLECTFUL ::
- A. cautious : reckless
- B. worried : problem
- C. fatigued : exhausted
- D. friendly : neighborly

____ 7. HEINOUS : MURDER ::
- A. swift : turtle
- B. minor : catastrophe
- C. destructive : tornado
- D. tragic : joke

____ 8. AUSPICIOUS : FOUR-LEAF CLOVER ::
- A. threatening : butterfly
- B. ominous : broken mirror
- C. time-consuming : toast
- D. disastrous : first prize

____ 9. INSINUATE : HINT ::
- A. hear : see
- B. exercise : jump rope
- C. express : communicate
- D. read : calculate

____ 10. INTERROGATE : QUESTION ::
- A. hide : see
- B. investigate : examine
- C. climb : descend
- D. know : guess

(Continues on next page)

____ 11. INCAPACITATE : BROKEN LEG ::
A. energize : flu
B. inform : sneeze
C. entertain : telephone book
D. delay : traffic jam

____ 12. HIERARCHY : LEVELS ::
A. closet : room
B. school : grades
C. petals : flowers
D. pain : medications

____ 13. PARAMOUNT : IMPORTANT ::
A. early : late
B. educational : recess
C. deadly : unhealthy
D. parallel : intersecting

____ 14. TURBULENT : WAR ::
A. evil : pear
B. few : pounds
C. tiny : atom
D. desirable : illness

____ 15. IMPROMPTU : PREPARED ::
A. lengthy : boring
B. gown : costume
C. planned : rehearsed
D. noisy : quiet

____ 16. INTUITION : HUNCH ::
A. instinct : skill
B. logic : deduction
C. hope : fear
D. invention : copy

____ 17. EXPEDITE : DELIVERY ::
A. extend : deadline
B. delay : departure
C. accelerate : automobile
D. credit : bill

____ 18. ABRASIVE : SCRATCH ::
A. large : nail
B. pliers : tool
C. sharp : cut
D. fork : spoon

____ 19. DERIDE : PRAISE ::
A. decide : ignore
B. divide : unite
C. appear : show up
D. deliver : package

____ 20. MACABRE : HORROR FILM ::
A. old-fashioned : website
B. amusing : math lecture
C. X-rated : sermon
D. useful : cookbook

Score (Number correct) ________ x 5 = ________%

Enter your score above and in the **Vocabulary Performance Chart** on the inside back cover of the book.

Appendixes

A. Limited Answer Key

IMPORTANT NOTE: Be sure to use this answer key as a learning tool only. You should not turn to this key until you have considered carefully the sentence in which a given word appears.

Used properly, the key will help you to learn words and to prepare for the activities and tests for which answers are not given. For ease of reference, the title of the "Final Check" passage in each chapter appears in parentheses.

Chapter 1 (Apartment Problems)

Sentence Check 1

1. scrupulous
2. gregarious
3. dexterous
4. detriment
5. discretion
6. facetious
7. sensory
8. optimum
9. vicarious
10. ostentatious

Chapter 2 (Hardly a Loser)

Sentence Check 1

1. venerate
2. zealot
3. instigate
4. despondent
5. rudimentary
6. resilient
7. retrospect
8. squelch
9. collaborate
10. scoff

Chapter 3 (Grandfather at the Art Museum)

Sentence Check 1

1. fritter
2. inadvertent
3. subsidize
4. sporadic
5. lethargy
6. inane
7. ambiguous
8. dissident
9. juxtapose
10. embellish

Chapter 4 (An Artist Named Vincent)

Sentence Check 1

1. estrange
2. relinquish
3. euphoric
4. zenith
5. regress
6. impetuous
7. maudlin
8. ubiquitous
9. berate
10. infallible

Chapter 5 (A Phony Friend)

Sentence Check 1

1. reprehensible
2. solicitous
3. predisposed
4. impeccable
5. solace
6. equivocate
7. liaison
8. fortuitous
9. propensity
10. sham

Chapter 6 (Coco the Gorilla)

Sentence Check 1

1. circumvent
2. robust
3. sanction
4. vociferous
5. oblivious
6. reticent
7. attrition
8. inundate
9. grievous
10. cohesive

Chapter 7 (Our Annual Garage Sale)

Sentence Check 1

1. tenet
2. depreciate
3. bolster
4. indiscriminate
5. terse
6. inquisitive
7. sedentary
8. nebulous
9. relegate
10. replete

Chapter 8 (My Large Family)

Sentence Check 1

1. contingency
2. indigenous
3. liability
4. reinstate
5. incongruous
6. egocentric
7. superfluous
8. clandestine
9. prolific
10. exonerate

Chapter 9 (A Costume Party)

Sentence Check 1

1. facsimile
2. grotesque
3. provocative
4. notorious
5. travesty
6. Metamorphosis
7. austere
8. perfunctory
9. mesmerize
10. esoteric

Chapter 10 (The Missing Painting)

Sentence Check 1

1. verbose
2. connoisseur
3. symmetrical
4. plight
5. contrite
6. superficially
7. lucid
8. distraught
9. germane
10. conspiracy

Chapter 11 (An Ohio Girl in New York)

Sentence Check 1

1. eradicate
2. stint
3. sordid
4. adept
5. presumptuous
6. standardize
7. entrepreneur
8. stringent
9. encompass
10. homogeneous

Chapter 12 (How Neat Is Neat Enough?)

Sentence Check 1

1. exhort
2. foible
3. masochist
4. magnanimous
5. repugnant
6. flamboyant
7. meticulous
8. recrimination
9. rancor
10. innocuous

Chapter 13 (Thomas Dooley)

Sentence Check 1

1. deplore
2. unprecedented
3. exacerbate
4. mitigate
5. deprivation
6. atrophy
7. imperative
8. panacea
9. objective
10. utilitarian

Chapter 14 (The Girl Who Fell from the Sky)

Sentence Check 1

1. exhilaration
2. exorbitant
3. rejuvenate
4. tenuous
5. decorum
6. orthodox
7. synchronize
8. espouse
9. extricate
10. facilitate

Chapter 15 (A Different Kind of Doctor)

Sentence Check 1

1. proficient
2. criterion
3. staunch
4. annihilate
5. subversive
6. placebo
7. vindicate
8. analogy
9. emanate
10. holistic

Chapter 16 (My Devilish Older Sister)

Sentence Check 1

1. retribution
2. interrogate
3. opportune
4. forestall
5. permeate
6. obsequious
7. insinuate
8. omnipotent
9. insidious
10. disparity

Chapter 17 (Harriet Tubman)

Sentence Check 1

1. discreet
2. impromptu
3. heinous
4. flout
5. intuition
6. obtrusive
7. inference
8. complement
9. fastidious
10. implement

Chapter 18 (Tony's Rehabilitation)

Sentence Check 1

1. redeem
2. expedite
3. fraudulent
4. transgress
5. subordinate
6. extenuating
7. innuendo
8. vehement
9. rebuke
10. auspicious

Chapter 19 (Rumors)

Sentence Check 1

1. derogatory
2. misconstrue
3. impending
4. paramount
5. macabre
6. deride
7. turbulent
8. quandary
9. validate
10. fabricate

Chapter 20 (Firing Our Boss)

Sentence Check 1

1. hierarchy
2. antithesis
3. incapacitate
4. abrasive
5. tumult
6. emulate
7. culmination
8. docile
9. prognosis
10. admonish

B. Dictionary Use

It isn't always possible to figure out the meaning of a word from its context, and that's where a dictionary comes in. Following is some basic information to help you use a printed or online dictionary.

How to Find a Word

A printed dictionary contains many thousands of words. But if you know how to use guidewords, you can find a word rather quickly. *Guidewords* are the two words at the top of each dictionary page. The first guideword tells what the first word is on the page. The second guideword tells what the last word is on that page. The other words on a page fall alphabetically between the two guidewords. So when you look up a word, find the two guidewords that alphabetically surround the word you're looking for.

● Which of the following pairs of guidewords would be on the page with the word *skirmish*? (The answer to this and the questions that follow appear on the next page.)

skimp / skyscraper **skyward / slave** **sixty / skimming**

If you have access to the internet, you can visit a dictionary website and type the word you want to look up. And some computer programs, such as Microsoft Word, offer built-in dictionary tools.

How to Use a Dictionary Listing

driz•zle (drĭz′əl) *v.* **-zled, -zling.** To rain gently and steadily in fine drops.
— *n.* A very light rain. —**driz′zly,** *adj.*

A dictionary listing includes many pieces of information, as shown in the above example for *drizzle*. Note that it provides much more than just a definition. Key parts include:

Syllables. Dots separate dictionary entry words into syllables. Note that *drizzle* has one dot, which breaks the word into two syllables.

● To practice seeing the syllable breakdown in a dictionary entry, write the number of syllables in each word below.

glam•our _____ **mi•cro•wave** _____ **in•de•scrib•a•ble** _____

Pronunciation guide. The information within parentheses after the entry word shows how to pronounce the entry word. This pronunciation guide includes two types of symbols: pronunciation symbols and accent marks.

Pronunciation symbols represent the consonant and vowel sounds in a word. The consonant sounds are probably very familiar to you, but you may find it helpful to review some of the sounds of the vowels—*a, e, i, o,* and *u*. Every dictionary has a key explaining the sounds of its pronunciation symbols, including the long and short sounds of vowels. (See the Pronunciation Guide on the inside front cover of this book.)

Long vowels have the sound of their own names. For example, the *a* in *pay* and the *o* in *no* both have long vowel sounds. Long vowel sounds are shown by a straight line above the vowel.

In many dictionaries, the *short vowels* are shown by a curved line above the vowel. Thus the *i* in the first syllable of *drizzle* is a short *i*. The pronunciation chart on the inside front cover of this book indicates that the short *i* has the sound of *i* in *ill*. It also indicates that the short *a* has the sound of *a* in *apple*, that the short *e* has the sound of *e* in *end*, and so on.

● Which of the words below have a short vowel sound? Which has a long vowel sound?

drug ________ **night** ________ **sand** ________

Another pronunciation symbol is the *schwa* (ə), which looks like an upside-down *e* and has an "uh" sound. It stands for certain rapidly spoken, unaccented vowel sounds, such as the *a* in *above*, the *e* in *item*, the *i* in *easily*, the *o* in *gallop*, and the *u* in *circus*. Here are three words that include the schwa sound:

in•fant (ĭn′fənt) **bum•ble** (bŭm′bəl) **de•liv•er** (dĭ-lĭv′ər)

- Which syllable in *drizzle* contains the schwa sound, the first or the second? ____________

Accent marks are small black marks that tell you which syllable to emphasize, or stress, as you say a word. An accent mark follows *driz* in the pronunciation guide for *drizzle,* which tells you to stress the first syllable of *drizzle*. Syllables with no accent mark are not stressed. Some syllables are in between, and they are marked with a lighter accent mark.

- Which syllable has the stronger accent in *sentimental*? ____________

sen•ti•men•tal (sĕn′tə-mĕn′tl)

Parts of speech. After the pronunciation key and before each set of definitions, the entry word's parts of speech are given. The parts of speech are abbreviated as follows:

noun—*n.* pronoun—*pron.* adjective—*adj.* adverb—*adv.* verb—*v.*

- The listing for *drizzle* shows that it can be two parts of speech. Write them below:

____________ ____________

Definitions. Words often have more than one meaning. When they do, each meaning is usually numbered in the dictionary. You can tell which definition of a word fits a given sentence by the meaning of the sentence. For example, the word *charge* has several definitions, including these two: **1.** To ask as a price. **2**. To accuse or blame.

- Show with a check ( ) which definition (1 or 2) applies in each sentence below:

The store charged me less for the blouse because it was missing a button. 1 ___ 2 ___

My neighbor has been charged with shoplifting. 1 ___ 2 ___

Other information. After the definitions in a listing, you may get information about the *origin* of a word. Such information about origins, also known as *etymology,* is usually given in brackets. And you may sometimes be given one or more synonyms or antonyms for the entry word. *Synonyms* are words that are similar in meaning to the entry word; *antonyms* are words that are opposite in meaning.

Which Dictionaries to Own

You will find it useful to own two recent dictionaries: a small paperback dictionary to carry to class and a hardbound dictionary, which contains more information than a small paperback version. Among the good dictionaries strongly recommended are both the paperback and the hardcover editions of the following: *The American Heritage Dictionary, The Random House College Dictionary,* and *Webster's New World Dictionary.*

Good online dictionaries include **www.ahdictionary.com** and **www.merriam-webster.com**.

Answers to the Dictionary Questions

Guidewords: *skimp/skyscraper*
Number of syllables: 2, 3, 5
Vowels: *drug, sand* (short); *night* (long)
Schwa: second syllable of *drizzle*
Accent: stronger accent on third syllable *(men)*
Parts of speech: noun and verb
Definitions: 1; 2

C. Topics for Discussion and Writing

NOTE: The first three items for each chapter are intended for discussion; the last three, for writing. Feel free, however, to either talk or write about any of the items.

Chapter 1 (Apartment Problems)

1. Athletes training for the Olympics must be **dexterous**. What are some of the other qualities—physical, emotional, and mental—necessary for them to achieve **optimum** results?

2. **Facetious** remarks often communicate serious ideas. An example is this comment by Mark Twain: "One of the most striking differences between a cat and a lie is that a cat has only nine lives." What is the serious meaning behind that remark? What might be the benefit of expressing that meaning in a joking manner?

3. Is it possible to be too **scrupulous** about following rules? Describe a situation in which someone, perhaps an authority figure, was more concerned with the rules than with the welfare of the people involved. Do you agree or disagree with that person's point of view? Explain your answer.

4. Write about a film that gave you an enjoyable **vicarious** experience. Name the film and describe at least one scene that illustrates your point. Begin with a main idea such as this: *The movie ________________ gave me a great vicarious experience of being a martial-arts expert.*

5. Did you ever wish you had used more **discretion**? For example, you may have told someone you disapproved of a mutual friend's behavior and later regretted doing so. Write a paper about what you said and why you later regretted saying it. Conclude by telling what you learned from the experience.

6. Who is your most **gregarious** friend or relative? Who is the most shy? In writing, contrast these two people by describing the different ways they react to at least two or three common circumstances, such as being at parties and choosing jobs. Use examples where possible.

Chapter 2 (Hardly a Loser)

1. Do you prefer to work alone on a project, such as a report, or to **collaborate** with others? What are the benefits and drawbacks of each way of working?

2. What are some ways parents and teachers **squelch** children's confidence and creativity? What can they do to encourage children to feel positive about themselves and their abilities?

3. Throughout the ages, **zealots** have **instigated** both good and bad events. What public person or personal acquaintance do you consider a zealot? What do you think makes this person a zealot? Has his or her attitude had good effects—or bad ones?

4. We **venerate** people in a wide variety of fields, from athletics and entertainment to military and religious organizations. Write about a public figure you greatly respect, describing and illustrating the qualities and/or abilities that make you respect this person.

5. Think of a time you behaved in a way that you later regretted. Write about how you acted and how, in **retrospect**, you feel you should have behaved.

6. Has anyone ever **scoffed** at a goal or plan of yours? Write a paper explaining your goal or plan, the other person's comments, and how you reacted. Did you become **despondent** and not follow through? Or were you **resilient** and able to move forward with your idea despite the disapproval?

Chapter 3 (Grandfather at the Art Museum)

1. Some parents and teachers feel that young people **fritter** away their time on text messaging and video games. Do you agree? Explain what you feel are the good or bad effects of either or both on young people.
2. What school activity do you wish a community organization would **subsidize**? Would you like a program giving students internships in various workplaces? A girls' boxing program? Or something else? Explain and defend the program you name.
3. Tell about a historical, political or religious **dissident** you admire. What did that person oppose? What did he or she achieve? Did the person suffer for his or her views and activities?
4. The ways we **embellish** spaces influence how they make us feel. For instance, a hospital waiting room may be designed to calm and comfort. Write a paper describing the decor of a room with which you're familiar and the effects you think it creates.
5. Write about a time you lost out on something (for example, a job) because of **lethargy**—you simply didn't get up enough energy to follow through. **Juxtapose** that story with an account of a time you pursued and achieved something you really wanted. Use this main idea: *Two very different experiences showed me that if I want something, I must take action.*
6. Have you ever made an **inadvertent** comment that was so **inane** you felt embarrassed afterward? Write a paper describing the incident and how you reacted when you realized what you had said.

Chapter 4 (An Artist Named Vincent)

1. Have you ever **relinquished** a social activity in order to do homework? Or have you ever ignored homework in favor of a social activity? Were you later glad you made the choice you did?
2. Young people may feel **infallible** and behave in **impetuous** and sometimes dangerous ways. What are some examples of such behavior? How might friends help these people avoid harmful, even tragic results?
3. Do you know anyone who has **regressed** to an earlier behavior? For example, you may know someone who began smoking again after having quit. Why do you think this person returned to the old behavior?
4. You have probably seen—or may have been—someone publicly **berated** at school, on the job, or in a chat room. Write a paper about such an incident and your reaction to it.
5. Has an argument or a misunderstanding ever **estranged** you from a relative or an old friend? In a paper, explain the situation and what you think can be done, or has been done, to repair the relationship.
6. For many actors, winning an Academy Award is the **zenith** of their career. **Euphoric**, they give emotional, sometimes even **maudlin**, speeches thanking others and describing their feelings. Think of an important goal you have achieved. Then write a speech—perhaps one humorously imitating an Academy Award speech—that you could have given upon reaching your goal.

Chapter 5 (A Phony Friend)

1. Some guests on television real-life talk shows become very emotional, even violent. Do you find such behavior **reprehensible**—or acceptable? In your opinion, are these demonstrations genuine, or are they mostly a **sham** and thus not to be taken seriously?

2. Politicians may **equivocate** when answering questions about controversial issues. Why do you think they do this? Can you think of any examples of such deliberate vagueness?

3. When there's a conflict between nations or between a union and a company, a **liaison** is generally called upon to help. Why do you think a go-between is used so often? Why don't the conflicting parties face each other without a mediator?

4. Sometimes when we're sad, a pet can give us **solace** when no one else can. Write a paper on the qualities that enable pets to offer such comfort, using examples you know of.

5. Do you know someone whose appearance or manners seem faultless? Do you consider a certain car or garden to be perfect? Write a paper in which you try to persuade your reader that someone or something is **impeccable**. Include colorful, convincing details in your description.

6. Write about someone who has a **propensity** to get into trouble. Include one or more detailed examples of his or her actions and the trouble that resulted. Also, explain why you think this person is **predisposed** to such situations. Use a main idea such as this: *My brother's habit of acting without thinking often gets him in trouble.*

Chapter 6 (Coco the Gorilla)

1. High-school and college coaches always lose players through **attrition**. What are some ways this happens? How, then, can a coach create a **cohesive** group of players and mold them into a winning team?

2. Have you ever felt **inundated** with school assignments? Describe study methods you have worked out to help you survive such difficult times. For instance, do you become super-organized? Do you read when you're on a bus?

3. Some students protest in a **vociferous** manner when required to dissect an animal. Do you think these students should be excused from the activity without being punished? Why or why not?

4. When parents divorce, they often fear **grievous** results for their children. But that depends on how contentious° the split is and how parents discuss it with their children. Some parents explain to their children why they've divorced, while others are **reticent**, feeling they are protecting the children by not giving the details of the breakup. Write a paper explaining which method you think is more helpful to a child and why.

5. We all want to be **robust**, yet we are sometimes **oblivious** to our own health practices. Think about your own diet and exercise patterns. Then write about two or three ways in which you can improve your chances for remaining healthy and strong.

6. Sometimes, even though we try to **circumvent** an unpleasant situation, we find we have no choice except to become involved. Has this ever happened to you or someone you know? In a paper, describe such a circumstance and what eventually happened.

Chapter 7 (Our Annual Garage Sale)

1. Television news is **replete** with images of violence and disaster. If you were in charge of news programming, would you balance negative news with reports meant to **bolster** viewers' spirits? If so, explain your reasoning and how you might achieve that balance. If not, explain why.

2. Some T-shirts or bumper stickers display **terse** statements that are serious or humorous. Which ones are your favorites? Is there one that particularly expresses a **tenet** by which you live?

3. Do you sometimes go through long periods of being quite **sedentary**? How can people include exercise in their study or work routines?

4. Some people collect items they hope won't **depreciate**, such as stamps. Others collect objects with little financial value, like refrigerator magnets. Do (or did) you or someone you know collect anything? Write a paper about the collection. How did it start? Which are its most prized items? Is it displayed, or has it been **relegated** to the basement?

5. Write a letter to a friend who has given only **nebulous** thought to a career and could end up making an **indiscriminate** career choice. Explain a way to go about choosing a satisfying occupation. Use some real or imagined examples to make your points clearer and more persuasive.

6. Imagine you are preparing a guide for camp counselors. One section of the guide must tell what to do in rainy weather, when children are stuck inside a room for hours. Write about three or more activities the counselor can lead to occupy the children's **inquisitive** minds and keep them from becoming bored and cranky.

Chapter 8 (My Large Family)

1. On holidays, does your family prepare **superfluous** amounts of food in case uninvited guests show up? Describe how you or relatives overprepare (or underprepare) for such a **contingency**.

2. What are some characteristics and behaviors of **egocentric** people? In what ways might self-centeredness be a **liability**—or an advantage?

3. When a defendant in a criminal trial has been **exonerated** of all charges, he or she is set free. What difficulties do you think this person might face in attempting to be **reinstated** into normal life?

4. While Native Americans are **indigenous** to North America, most Americans have roots in other countries. Write a paper on your family's roots and movements from place to place. Trace your family as far back as you can.

5. A friendship between people who appear completely different from each other may seem **incongruous**. Do you know of such a friendship? Write a paper explaining the relationship and the qualities that seem contradictory. Tell what you think draws the friends to each other.

6. Have you ever had to behave in a **clandestine** manner to keep a surprise secret? Write about the surprise and what you had to do to hide it. Here's a sample main idea for this assignment: *Because of a surprise party, I had to become a creative liar.*

Chapter 9 (A Costume Party)

1. Schools adopt dress code policies to prevent students from wearing "inappropriate," or **provocative**, clothes to school. What are some rules of dress in the school you attend or once attended? Do you support dress codes in schools?

2. Mary Shelley's novel *Frankenstein,* the story of a scientist and his **grotesque** creation, has been made into a film several times. Why do you think this story continues to **mesmerize** people?

3. One company makes perfect **facsimiles** of famous paintings, down to the brushstrokes. The copies are sold for much less than the originals. Similarly, laboratory-produced gems are much cheaper than those found in nature. Why do you think people value the originals more than the less expensive copies?

4. Do you study best in a quiet, **austere** environment or a noisy, cluttered space—or something in between? Write a paper on the study setting you prefer. Describe the setting in detail, and tell why you feel it works for you.

5. Some students give only **perfunctory** attention to what happens in class. Write a letter to a teacher telling two or three ways class can be made more interesting for such students.

6. Write the first page or two of a short story, realistic or otherwise, about a **notorious** criminal who tries to undergo a **metamorphosis** in order to escape being recognized and caught by crimefighters.

Chapter 10 (The Missing Painting)

1. Group study can be helpful, but conversations may spring up that aren't **germane** to the study material. Do you prefer to study with friends or by yourself? Or does it depend on the circumstances? Discuss the pros and cons of both study methods, and give reasons for your preferences.

2. Even when people feel **contrite** about something they did, their apology may sound more like an excuse than regret. Think of examples. Why do you think it is difficult for some people to apologize?

3. To avoid being a **verbose** writer, watch for and eliminate unnecessary words. For practice, edit the following statements so that each is only four words: "Hattie was elected to the position of secretary." "At this point in time, I have need of a nap." "I really prefer the dark kind of chocolate." Why might **connoisseurs** of writing recommend this technique?

4. Were you ever so concerned about personal matters that you paid attention only **superficially** to your studies? Were you **distraught** when your limited studying led to low grades? Write about what prevented you from doing well in school and how things turned out.

5. Smartphones and social media are changing how people get their news. Is this change good or bad? For example, can the **plight** of vulnerable people be aided by this new source of information? Write a **lucid** paragraph in which you argue for or against social media and its impact on our news.

6. Sometimes when nothing seems to go right, we may feel as though there's a **conspiracy** against us. Has this ever happened to you? Write about your experience and how it turned out.

Chapter 11 (An Ohio Girl in New York)

1. Celebrity gossip sites are **adept** at appealing to people's interest in **sordid** events. Why do you think people are so attracted to the information these websites offer?

2. Has a **stint** at a part-time or full-time job ever turned into a horrible experience for you? What were the circumstances? Did you quit the job or stick with it?

3. Schools and colleges in most states **standardize** the tests and instruction they provide students. What do you think are the benefits and drawbacks of requiring students to learn—and be tested on— the same material?

4. Some teachers have **stringent** standards, while others are easier to satisfy. Write a paper contrasting strict and lenient teachers. Explain, for instance, the differences in their assignments and grading methods. Also tell which type of teacher you prefer and why. You might use the following main idea: *In my experience, a __________ teacher is generally preferable to a __________ one.*

5. Write a paper explaining which habit you would choose to **eradicate** if you could, and why. Go on to name two or three realistic methods you could use to get rid of, or at least weaken, that habit.

6. Imagine you are an **entrepreneur** opening a restaurant chain. Write a description of your business. Include the restaurant's name, theme, decor, and a general description of what the menu would **encompass**.

Chapter 12 (How Neat Is Neat Enough?)

1. When you were a child, did your parents **exhort** you to eat foods you found **repugnant**? What were these foods, and what did you do, if anything, to avoid eating them? How do you feel about these foods today?

2. People's **foibles**, though **innocuous**, can sometimes annoy others. What foibles do your roommates or family members have that sometimes irritate you? Which of your foibles annoy others?

3. Are you **meticulous** about keeping your room and belongings neat, or are you more casual with your environment? Describe what your classmates would see if they were to enter your room right now.

4. Do you know, or know of, someone who is truly **magnanimous**? In a paper, describe that person and tell what he or she has done to deserve your opinion.

5. Sometimes people have an argument that escalates into ongoing **recriminations** and **rancor** that can last for years. Write a paper describing such a conflict and explaining what you think might be done to ease it.

6. Imagine a fictitious person who is very **flamboyant**. Write a paper describing this person's showy appearance and behavior. Also tell what this flamboyance might indicate about his or her nature.

Chapter 13 (Thomas Dooley)

1. When you were a child, did a special treat work as a **panacea** to cure emotional upsets? Is there a certain activity today—listening to music or talking to someone special—that you can count on to lift your blue moods?

2. Being **objective** is **imperative** for a judge and a jury, but it is also important in other areas of life. What are some situations when it's important for people to be objective? For instance, is objectivity important in hiring an employee? In choosing friends?

3. We are surrounded by **utilitarian** things: pencils, light switches, doorknobs, and so on. What are some objects that are *not* utilitarian and are kept solely for aesthetic reasons? Now name some utilitarian things that are both attractive *and* useful.

4. No matter how much we like television, many of us **deplore** something about it. We may feel that it promotes poor values or that local news shows care more about ratings than news. Write a paper on what you most disapprove of about TV. Include detailed examples.

5. Did someone who tried to help you with a problem actually **exacerbate** the situation? Write about what happened and how you eventually handled your problem.

6. Have you ever worn a cast? How badly did your muscles **atrophy** while in the cast? Was physical therapy used to **mitigate** the muscle weakness? Write a paper about your experience. Tell why you needed to wear the cast and what problems or inconveniences you experienced while wearing it and after removing it.

Chapter 14 (The Girl Who Fell from the Sky)

1. When stressful situations leave you exhausted, do you wish you could get away for a while? If you could take an all-expenses-paid two-week vacation, where would you go, and what would you do to **rejuvenate** yourself?

2. Some people feel **exhilaration** when running five miles, whereas others feel it from beating a difficult computer game. What activity fills you with excitement? Explain its appeal to you.

3. What is the worst mess you've ever gotten yourself into? Have you ever made two appointments or dates for the same time and day, or agreed to do something and later wished you hadn't? Describe the situation, and explain how you managed to **extricate** yourself.

4. Have you ever been criticized by someone who **espoused** what you consider an old-fashioned sense of **decorum**? For instance, has a relative insisted that nose piercing is crude or that it's wrong for females to call males for a date? Write a paper about your experience. Describe the situation, the other person's opinion, and your own point of view and reaction.

5. Did you ever want something so much that you paid what seemed like an **exorbitant** price for it? After the purchase, did you still feel it was worth what you paid? Do you or does someone you gave the item to still own it? Write about your experience. Be sure to describe what you bought in a way that shows your reader why you were willing to pay so much for it.

6. Imagine you write an advice column. A tenth grader who has moved to a new school district asks for your ideas on how to **facilitate** his or her adjustment to the new school. For your column, write a letter to that person.

Chapter 15 (A Different Kind of Doctor)

1. Some patients who receive **placebos** (instead of real medications) report good results, even cures. What do you think could account for these results?

2. Throughout history, the power of persuasion **emanated** from some people so strongly that they were able to influence masses of people. Name some of those people. Did any of them use their abilities for **subversive** purposes? Explain.

3. In focusing on the whole person, what might **holistic** physicians do that other doctors often do not do? For instance, what life changes might they suggest?

4. Are you a **staunch** fan of a particular sports team? Write a paper explaining what you like about that team. Give examples for all your claims.

5. Were you ever wrongly accused of doing something? If so, were you able to **vindicate** yourself? Write a paper explaining the accusation and its effects upon you. Describe in detail the way you were—or were not—cleared of blame. Feel free to use this main idea: *I learned the hard way how important it is to be careful in making accusations.*

6. Are you good at tennis? An expert baker? Write a paper on an activity in which you feel especially **proficient**. Describe the skill, and tell how you came to acquire it and what place it occupies in your life now. Conclude by explaining whether you intend to use the skill in a career or as a hobby.

Chapter 16 (My Devilish Older Sister)

1. Do you dislike certain activities, such as exercise or doing laundry, so much that you find ways to **forestall** doing them? Tell which activities you dislike, why you dislike them so much, and what delaying actions you take.

2. Did your parents ever ask you questions like "Where are you going?" and "Who else will be there?" How do young people react to being **interrogated** in this fashion? Are those reactions justified? Why or why not?

3. Do wonderful odors **permeate** your home at certain times of the year, such as particular holidays or seasons? Identify the aromas and the special times with which you associate them.

4. Has anything happened to you at a particularly **opportune** time? For instance, did you get a job offer just when you needed more money? Did you meet someone special right after breaking up with someone else? Write a paper describing one such time in your life, making clear just why the timing of the event was so good. Alternatively, write about an inopportune, or ill-timed, event in your life.

5. Are you good friends with someone despite **disparities** in your opinions, ages, and/or backgrounds? Write about your relationship, explaining the differences between you and how you both handle them so that your friendship is maintained. Has anyone **insinuated** that your friendship is inappropriate? If so, also tell how you dealt with the objection.

6. Have you ever wished to be **omnipotent**? Write a paper describing what you would do and why if you were all-powerful for a day. Include any **retributions** you would like to give out.

Chapter 17 (Harriet Tubman)

1. Imagine you are asked right now to give an **impromptu** speech defending this point: Sports help society. Give one example, fact, or personal experience you could use to support that point.

2. When you get dressed in the morning, are you **fastidious** about choosing accessories to **complement** your outfit? Or are you more casual about your day's attire? Picture this outfit: black shirt, black pants, and black shoes. Name one piece of clothing or jewelry for a male or a female that you feel would complement that outfit.

3. Do you trust your instincts? Tell about a time when you did *not* follow your **intuition** and wished that you had, or a time you *did* follow your instincts and you were, or were not, glad you did.

4. On New Year's Day, many people decide to begin a self-improvement program. The **inference** is that if they make a New Year's resolution, they will stick with the plan, yet it is often soon forgotten. Have you ever made a resolution (at any time of the year) and actually followed through? Write a paper explaining the resolution and how you **implemented** it. Or write about a resolution you might make in the future and the ways you could carry it out.

5. Have you ever asked a friend or family member to be **discreet** about some information and then discovered it was told to others? Write a paper about your experience and how you handled it.

6. Write the first page or two of a novel about an evil character who **flouts** society's rules. Describe the character and a **heinous** plan he or she is working on.

Chapter 18 (Tony's Rehabilitation)

1. Judges sometimes require people who have **transgressed** but are not violent to **redeem** themselves by doing community work. Do you think community work is a fair punishment? What are the advantages and disadvantages of such a penalty?

2. Some people believe that their astrological signs are **auspicious** at certain times and plan their days accordingly. Do you believe in astrology? Give your opinion and the reasons you feel as you do.

3. What do you do to **expedite** unpleasant chores such as housecleaning or yard work? Explain your methods and why they are helpful to you.

4. Have **extenuating** circumstances ever caused you to miss an important test or appointment? Write a paper about the experience. Describe the circumstances, the reaction to your missing the test or appointment, and what happened in the end.

5. Did you ever harshly **rebuke** someone and later regret it and try to remedy the situation? Write a paper about the experience. Or write about a time you were at the receiving end of **vehement** criticism and what responses, if any, you made to the **derogatory** remarks.

6. What kind of boss would you want to be? Imagine that you are a boss and have asked the workers **subordinate** to you to evaluate your performance anonymously. Write an evaluation you would like to see.

Chapter 19 (Rumors)

1. What do you think are the reasons **macabre** movies are so popular? Give some examples. What do *you* think of such movies, and how do you respond to them?
2. Children sometimes **fabricate** stories, especially when they think they've done something that might get them into trouble. How do you think parents should handle this behavior?
3. Some people are frightened by **turbulent** storms, while others enjoy a lot of lightning and thunder. What is your reaction to violent weather? If you have a pet, how does it react to thunderstorms?
4. Have you ever been in a **quandary** because you wanted to do something your family disapproved of? For example, you might have wanted to buy a car, but your parents wanted you to use the money for college. Write a paper explaining the predicament and the decision you made.
5. Has anyone ever **derided** or criticized something that was of **paramount** importance to you, such as your choice of friends, jobs, or extracurricular activities? Write about the experience, including how you reacted to the ridicule or criticism.
6. Write a paper in which you **validate** one of the following italicized statements with at least two persuasive pieces of evidence—facts, examples, or reasons from your personal experience and common sense. *About everything bad there is something good. Parents coddle their children too much nowadays. Music classes benefit students.*

Chapter 20 (Firing Our Boss)

1. Is there someone you would like to **emulate**? The person might be someone you know, a famous individual, or a character in a novel or film. Tell how you'd like to be similar to that person and why.
2. Some people like to work for a large company with a structured **hierarchy**. Others prefer to work for a small business with a more casual structure. Which of these work settings best suits your temperament and career plans? Why?
3. Do you know a couple who are the **antithesis** of one another? For instance, is your uncle very sociable and your aunt shy? Is one person in the couple **abrasive** and the other **docile**? Despite their differences, do the two people seem well suited to each other? Why or why not?
4. Has a politician, athlete, or other public person done something you strongly disapprove of? Write a letter to that person in which you **admonish** him or her and suggest a better behavior.
5. Imagine you are a counselor. Write a professional report about someone who is **incapacitated** by extreme shyness. Describe the person and tell what you think should be done to help him or her. Conclude with what the **prognosis** would be if your program is followed.
6. Graduation day is the **culmination** of years of academic, social, and athletic experiences. Imagine that you are giving a speech at your graduation ceremony. What are some memories you would share with your classmates? What are some words of advice you would give them? Write the speech you would give.

D. Word List

Notes

Notes

Notes

Notes

Notes

Notes